Helen Martin is truly a wo
outdoorswoman . . . with a quick wit and full measure of that rarest
virtue, common sense. It's been my privilege to know her for more than . . .
well, for a lot of years . . . but I have never known the actress or the model.
I only knew Helen, a serious huntress whether in high mountains or dense
forests. . . . Turns out she has quite a story to tell . . . and isn't afraid to tell
stories on herself.

—Craig Boddington—
Outdoor Journalist, Television Show Host, Award-Winning Author

When you are a Skrebneski model . . . you are not only beautiful but also
extremely professional.

—Victor Skrebneski—
Groundbreaking American Fashion Photographer and Author

Fashion icon Helen Martin's style sense is in her DNA whether she is on the
runway or exploring the out-of-doors. Her book is a great read—exciting and
amusing stories as she takes you behind the scenes of the modeling industry.

—Lisa Dawson—
President, Kim Dawson Agency

Helen Martin's book, *High Fashion, High Adventure,* takes you to places that
you only imagine. Her experiences are not only adventurous, but exist in the
realms of reality being truly more fascinating than fiction. Her stories are
poignant, funny, and human, exploring the magic of life. The dichotomy of
her unique experiences are illuminated, as much as they are connected,
by her distinctive voice.

—Jill K. Sayre—
Author of *The Fairies of Turtle Creek*

HIGH FASHION
HIGH ADVENTURE

Helen Martin

HIGH FASHION HIGH ADVENTURE

The opinions expressed by the author are not necessarily those
of Wisdom House Books, Inc.

Published by Wisdom House Books, Inc.
Chapel Hill, North Carolina 27514 USA
1.919.883.4669 | www.wisdomhousebooks.com

Wisdom House Books is committed to excellence in the publishing industry.

Cover and Interior design by Ted Ruybal

Published in the United States of America

Paperback ISBN: 978-1-7320754-0-5
LCCN: 2018961617

1. BIO026000 | BIOGRAPHY & AUTOBIOGRAPHY / Personal Memoirs

2. BIO005000 | BIOGRAPHY & AUTOBIOGRAPHY / Entertainment & Performing Arts

First Edition
14 13 12 11 10 / 10 9 8 7 6 5 4 3 2 1

Table of Contents

"One should either be a work of art,
or wear a work of art"

—Oscar Wilde

On Discovering Style

I am not sure when I first truly understood the word 'style.' When I was very young, we wore dresses—light cotton dresses with flowers that fluttered and moved around our knees. Our tanned legs and arms were always in motion. We wore sturdy shoes with socks or white sandals with straps that buckled. Our long hair was always falling around our faces, sometimes held back with bobby pins or plastic barrettes. Mostly, I looked at women as beautiful and men as handsome. That was a time when men and women followed the styles of glamorous movie stars, copying their looks from hairstyles to dresses to peek-a-boo-toe shoes. My mother and her friends always looked like Hollywood screen goddesses to me. Born and educated in Italy, my mother had a definite European flair. She loved fashion, designing and sewing many of her clothes as well as ours.

On the evenings my parents were going out, my sisters and I would wait in the front foyer to watch them walk down the stairs: my father, handsome and debonair, always looked well dressed and put together. He loved clothes, often arriving home carrying a shopping bag, holding one more jacket. He literally collected them. I remember one especially—a tan flat wool, patch pockets, notch collar, large brown leather buttons—the same look Frank Sinatra and other stars wore in those shimmering, black-and-white 40s and 50s movies with so much allure. My mother, always resplendent, her hair freshly combed out after all day in pincurls, would descend the stairs, her red lips forming a perfect smile. I remember one dinner dress, a satin one-piece pencil skirt paired with a long-sleeve top with a lace insert across the bodice. If she added the lace, fully gathered, detachable skirt, open in the front and fastened with a satin ribbon, we knew there would be dancing. Off they would go to Lake Bracken Country Club or Harbor Lights Supper Club in Galesburg, Illinois. Years later, I produced several charity shows at Harbor Lights with my model friends from Chicago.

One of my early professional encounters with a living legend came in the form of Pauline Trigère, a leading designer in the industry. Who hasn't watched *Breakfast at Tiffany's* and admired the powerful, sophisticated wardrobe of Patricia Neal's character? That's Trigère. She was famous for her design technique—draping and cutting fabric directly on her models. I became one of those privileged models. My professional work and lifelong friendship with her started at the original Stanley Korshak store on Michigan Avenue in Chicago. By that time, I was an established fashion print and runway model, and Korshak had booked me for a Pauline Trigère Fall show.

After the show, she asked me to come to New York and be her design model for her next Spring Collection. It was a dream come true—to be working with one of the greatest American designers in fashion. Prior to her offer, I had been booked several times a year by my Chicago agent for photo shoots in New York, so I knew the city and loved it.

That initial period I spent with her was one of several coming-of-age experiences. She truly launched my understanding of how and what the fashionable woman should be; she embodied grace, elegance, and femininity and had a sensual quality that as a young—yet highly self-aware—model I was just starting to grasp.

There were three full-time design models, each one chosen to bring a certain "feel" to the collection. We would be ensconced in the models' room, talking and keeping up with fashion magazines. The day of the summons by cell phone had not yet arrived.

The draping session would start with me standing in my strapless bra with waist cinch and half slip in front of a mirrored wall. Trigère and I looked at each other, chatting as she attached temporary straps to my bra. She had chosen the fabric already from the dozens of fabric rolls behind us, some of her own design, others chosen from mills all over the world; her assistant sketched the design as she created it. Pinning and draping, cutting into a $300 per yard fabric, molding and shaping until she had what she wanted. All this took place in twenty minutes or so. I was undressed, thanked very graciously, and the garment would be placed on a mannequin for her to rework. I would be called back later in the same day, or in another day or so, to continue finessing the final design, after which there followed an animated discussion with Trigère's pattern man. Off it would come, and the garment would be immediately ushered to the pattern room.

I can still hear her voice when a piece was presented to her for the first inspection if it did not meet her exacting expectations. "This is not the work of the house of Trigère!" she would declare, while shaking the daylights out of the errant garment. It was all about drama at the prestigious Seventh Avenue showroom.

And then several weeks later came the excitement of the opening of my first New York showroom presentation. Seated in the reserved seats were buyers from major department stores, including Neiman Marcus, Bergdorf Goodman, Marshall Field, and Saks Fifth Avenue, plus many independent specialty stores from around the country—all of them bought Trigère. Stars and celebrities were always in attendance as well. Barbara Streisand was in the audience for a showing—I believe it was the following Fall collection—and afterward I modeled dresses for her. She appeared bigger than life on screen, but in person, she was petite, almost fragile, and certainly shy. I felt like a giant, looming over her showing the Trigère gowns.

Backstage, of course, is frantic during a show. Pauline calls for her Shalimar, which magically appears from the hands of Jimmy, one of the many design interns she mentors.

Pauline holds the bottle high and sprays the room, saying, "So you will feel beautiful." Shalimar is my perfume of choice to this day. A single dresser outfits each girl, sending them off to be checked by Pauline for a final "look-see," which will involve pinning a rose to a lapel or attaching one of her dozens of gold turtle pins to a jacket or a dress bodice. Then a smile and a touch on your shoulder and out into the spotlight to walk your walk, remembering the way you carry yourself on the runway in Chicago is the reason she brought you to her showroom in New York. I try not to disappoint.

I became one of the privileged: models and friends who were invited to a weekend at her country home, La Tortue [the turtle]. On the afternoon of the last day, we were relaxing on blankets by her pool after a swim, when I realized Pauline was removing her bathing suit nearby. Stretching and wiggling out of her suit while lying under a beach towel, she got naked, while we young-uns, male and female, watched in awe. When she was quite finished, she pulled the beach towel around her, swept off the blanket, leaving her wet suit where she had dropped it, and, turning, she walked up the small incline to the house. We were left staring at her crumpled suit. There was only one prima donna when Pauline was around, and it was she. May you rest in peace, dear Pauline.

Working with designers like Pauline Trigère in New York and James Galanos at Marshall Field's 28 Shop in Chicago, and later on the couture floor of Neiman Marcus's downtown flagship store in Dallas with the legendary Stanley Marcus looking on, was a privilege; these icons of fashion taught me that style is a way of being, the way you express yourself, how you move—style is the way in which you claim your space. A presence.

Givenchy, Valentino, Armani, Balenciaga: elegant, gorgeous men of style and genius. It was an honor to work with them. Oscar de la Renta, handsome and always so playful—he made every show fun. Karl Lagerfield, who checked me out before I stepped onto the stage of the Majestic Theater in Dallas, touched my arm and said how pleased he was that I was wearing his design.

My advice to women has always been: whatever you are doing, wherever you are going—think style, think glamour. When you walk into your closet to dress in the morning, if you do not see something that describes (screams!) those words—then ditch everything and start over. You only need one or two attractive, stylish items to make you feel good— like a belt. I bought a wide leather Michael Kors belt when he first came on the scene years ago; I wore it until it literally fell off me. But the glamorous element of an outfit can be a handbag, a wrap, a pair of French-cut jeans, a pencil skirt, that long fringed scarf, that vintage rhinestone cuff your Aunt Catherine gave you. All of it denotes style and glamour.

And glamour is everywhere. All around us. The Highland green-heather capes of Scotland, the French beret, a London Fog trench coat, Italian shoewear— and who isn't just a little thrilled to see the mounted men in blue, in full uniform, black boots polished to a high shine, astride a chestnut horse in upper Manhattan?

Every nation has their own culture brands.

The style up and down the length of Africa is astonishing—a wonder. Before I traveled to Uganda for the first time, I studied photographs and illustrations of tribal costumes and dress, but then to see them come alive in their own world was like watching an endless series of one-act plays. Watching the fashions parade by was a favorite pastime. I admired the creative ingenuity of Ugandans in following tribal custom and still creating a personal style.

I was fascinated with the young Karamojong women of Uganda, sashaying by in their short, layered skirts of leather, soft as cloth with edges raw and unhemmed. In spite of their long hours of physical labor, be it gathering firewood or toting water or tending animals, they dressed to please themselves. They wore colorful beads and bangles around their wrists, piles of necklaces, huge hoop earrings, a minute piece of material to cover their bosoms, and sometimes carried a child strapped over one shoulder, all the while toting hollowed-out decorated gourds filled with water.

When I first encountered the Herero women of Namibia, I was awestruck. Three stately women glided toward me dressed in their long, Victorian-style dresses, each silhouette and ensemble a work of art. There was nothing else for me to do but to stop and acknowledge them with a slight bow, hands pressed together against my chest, so I wouldn't start clapping or doing something inappropriate. They continued walking, and as they passed me, each gave a little nod my way. Their headdresses are uniquely African, with cloth of every design and color wrapped in a flat wide crown around their heads, breathtaking in the creative execution and unerring attention to detail.

Ah, and the Masai warriors—the men who have the last word in style and image! Their red robes flow around them, beautifully adorned with beaded necklaces and colorful cuffs around wrists and arms, as they confidently march across the plains carrying their staffs and spears, seeking new grass and water supplies for the tribe's herds of cattle and goats. In Kenya we were camped not far from the their bomas (*kraals*) so, of course, the warriors would come visit—checking everything out, walking around, staying just a few minutes, and invariably, two or more of the men would inspect themselves in our jeep's mirrors. Satisfied with what they saw, they departed as quietly as they had arrived.

The title for this little volume—*High Fashion, High Adventure*—was inspired by the stories I wrote as I pursued high fashion and high adventure (literally, I climbed mountains), uniting the two major themes of my life. Style is the thread that links all the essays together. *High Fashion, High Adventure* ends, appropriately, with a chapter dedicated to my style philosophy, happily offered here for your consideration. Use it wisely.

Definitely, the most wretched part of the whole modeling process in couture—long before, lights, music, go!—is the sacred beginning: the so-called fitting. As in, "you have a fitting at Neimans for Oscar de la Renta," Dottie at the agency would inform me, or the call could be for Valentino, Givenchy, Bill Blass, or Donna Karan.

Alrighty, then, I would decide. I can't have desert tonight, gotta go with salads, can't stop at McDonalds for a hamburger. I never dieted, really. I pretty much ate whatever I wanted, only very small portions. I knew a glorious platinum model friend of mine who would order a hamburger at the drivethrough, eat half on the way home, and then run in and shove the remaining half down the disposal. That was pretty much the way I dieted. During Spring and Fall fashion seasons, we were heavily booked, three to four jobs per day. Running from one location to another, the activity alone kept our weight in check. The day I quit modeling is the same day I gained ten pounds, I am sure of it, because I have been trying to lose the same ten pounds for years.

Dozens and dozens of fittings in many models' rooms, store fashion departments, designers' studios, hotel ballrooms and the infamous all night "paper fittings" backstage at the Dallas Apparel Mart.

But the designers' fittings at the original Stanley Korshak on Michigan Avenue in Chicago and the 28 Shop at Marshall

Field's in Chicago's Loop, and the fittings with Daria at Neiman's in downtown Dallas, did bring on the butterflies; anxieties doubled when you were being fitted in front of a world-class designer. I would say there would be a little anxiety all around, even with the highly professional Daria supervising; it was never talked about or mentioned. We retained total composure, presenting our most "model self" for scrutiny.

There are no alterations to a sample piece. If a piece does not "work" on one of us, the next model will wear it. Your hope is that you will fit into enough pieces to make the show. Because the fashion coordinators know each of us so well, they will try to book only the models that they know will fit a certain designer's collection. Sometimes it doesn't work. I have seen a designer reject models at the fitting because her look is wrong for him or her. It is the same way an actor is rejected, not because he or she hasn't the talent, but because the actor just isn't right for the part.

I was rejected once at a fitting at the Beverly Hills Hotel for an up-and-coming designer. I did not have the "California look." Really! My resume reads as follows, sir—Hair: brunette; Eyes: brown. He wanted blondes and redheads. Please, get over yourself.

Contemporary women of style inspire us everywhere today as well as glamorous women that reach out to us online from decades past. Michelle Persad recently reported: "If you look up the definition of 'style icon,' we think there should be a photo of Bianca Jagger next to the term." I so agree. I

Googled her style evolution just to see, one more time, that white wedding suit she wore when she and Mick married. A white fitted jacket, notch collar, over a long white A-line skirt, and the hat! A stunning wide-brimmed picture hat with flowing veil attached—The Lady in White.

Married in 1971, the Nicaragua-born beauty became one of the preeiment stylesetters of her day. I remember another hat she wore in the early 70s—the black, fitted cloche with a black veil to her chin and the highlight: a stack of snow white feathers attached to the crown and sweeping down almost to her shoulder.

Stylish, beautiful and glamorous women, like Bianca Jagger or Sophia Loren, retain their natural grace through the years because when they reach their later decades and beyond, they let nature deal with the years and their advancing age instead of trying to turn back the clock, which often ends with disastrous results. And why do younger men want to be with these older glamorous women? Because they are interesting, have tons of stories to tell, and, as my photographer friend, Carolyn Collins, tells it, they show exuberance and a flirty wisdom.

And where am I going with this?

Ah, here it is! Beauty really does come from within.

Although, it was really difficult to live by this motto and feel beautiful while wearing a Three-Piece Polyester, Double-Knit Pantsuit during its heyday. For those of you who might remember, perfectly fashionable women started buying these monstrosities in the 1970s. I know because I was paid thousands of dollars to be photographed in them during my modeling career. All my pictures in those double knits are stunning; I was accessorized beautifully, photographed in wonderful settings: at trendy restaurants, high-end hotels, and in lush parks; and yet, I could never bring myself to actually purchase one. Why? Because the fabric was not real—it was faux fabric. Those ridiculous sleeveless shells were cut by machines, with the fabric stacked ten layers deep. The bust darts fell somewhere around your breast line—if you were lucky. Fabric must move with your body line, feel good against your skin. It was not a good thing that when one removed the three-piece wonders, there was no need to hang the garment on a hanger. Look, I can stand it up in the corner!

We had incredible, talented and innovative designers during that time—people like Bob Mackie, Laura Ashley, Halston, Calvin Klein, Jordache. We had minis, middies, and maxis in every color and graphic design imaginable. And disco!

Unfortunately, another curse has come upon the land in recent years. Leggings. In reality, the so-called leggings I am referring to are not leggings at all—they're TIGHTS, the same old things we used to wear and still do wear to our work-outs. A profitable online industry has emerged, with TV shows and infomercials encouraging women of all shapes and sizes to don skin-tight leggings and just add a clever top. Are they insane?

Have we lost all sense of appropriateness, of image and style, of what a flattering silhouette means? Hopefully not, because we have the amazing Jennifer Lopez, or J-Lo, to define style. Some time back, the ultimate, on point fashion publication W did a photo shoot with her, taking her back to the Bronx and "the street where she lived." Elizabeth Taylor's performance in *Butterfield 8* inspired the photos, which are, of course, amazing. My favorites are the black and whites—they remind me of the nationally recognized fashion photographer Victor Skrebneski's early work in the 60s. More on him later. The color shot in Marc Jacob's dress and bolero is definitely something to write home about, however. She has certain poise, a strong presence and an intimate sexuality.

Hollywood glamour—the movies! Sitting in a darkened theater, becoming part of a make-believe world of adventure, culture and style. Oh, the clothes! I fell in love with the wedding dress Katherine Hepburn wore in *High Society*. White silk organdy with that white belt wrapped around her waist: total allure. And the most beautiful gown of this past decade, the infamous "green dress" Keira Knightly wore in *Atonement*. The gown is so feminine, with the accented low hip line and the sensuous flow of the fabric against her legs as she walked. Remarkable.

Who can forget David Bowie wearing McQueens's Union Jack frock coat for a 1997 concert? In April of 2015, before his death, I wrote in my blog that David Bowie is, for me, the essence of style. A career of musical innovation marked by continual re-invention, I loved him the most for his striking visual presence—not to mention his brilliant mind. So many greats have left us, but not their legacy, not their creative genius. We have all the best parts of them in their work.

We are in the midst of a "New Power Dressing" as related

by Vanessa Friedman, style editor, in several of her columns for the *New York Times*:

> This is one kind of aesthetic reaction, but not the only one. It is not only about hemlines, for example, at least not in the vein of Newtonian fashion physics (everything that goes up must come down). It's not about power dressing in the old, battering-ram-shoulder sense, but in the sense that when you feel secure and comfortable and protected, you feel stronger. It is reflected in both the hip historiana of Giambattista Valli's floral silk chiffons with their long sleeves, sweeping skirts and chaste necks, and the head-to-toe character-actor dressing at Gucci. In the boho Puritan lines of Pierpaolo Piccioli's Valentino and the slouchy tailoring of Stella McCartney, the elegant rock-star suiting of Haider Ackermann and the wind-swept Victorian romance of Erdem. Also the swaddling chic of Michael Kors.[1]

My Italian-born parents embraced the core concept of *la bella figura*, combining fashion and good manners. Later I would have the privilege to work with extraordinary people like Stanley Marcus, the arbiter of good taste, who understood that style went beyond the surface—it is about cutting a beautiful figure however and wherever life leads you.

---

1. 6 April 2017, "Women, Fashion Has You Covered," *New York Times*.

Photograph by Jeannette Korab

Photograph by Ron Pawelkowski, Hair Style by Fredrick Glaser

HELEN MARTIN

Photograph by Ron Pawelkowski, Head Costume by William Lutes

Photographed for the Mannequin Guild Ball (while President of the Guild) in Pauline Trigère

Fashion by Stephen Burrows, Photograph by Tom Purin

Photographed at the Drake Hotel, Chicago, Illinois, in fashion by designer Walter Holmes

Photographed in Chicago, Illinois, in Walter Holmes's Black & White
Collection

Marshall Field's Fashion Show, Chicago, Illinois

Who's Your Agent?

Photographer Kenneth Heilbron booked me for my first fashion print job. It was a very big deal.

He was one of the photographers shooting a couture show in the 28 Shop at Marshall Field in downtown Chicago. He approached me after taking my picture for the fashion sections of the city's newspapers.

When the couture show ended, he said he wanted to book me for a print job and added, "Who is your agent?"

I said, "I don't have an agent," as a little flutter of fear ran through my tummy.

He responded, "That's fine, here's my phone number, call me, I'll give you the particulars." I was stunned, excited, happy and very, very nervous at the same time.

He wanted me for a paid photo shoot, not just for a candid after a fashion show where we were only paid for the show and the fittings—albeit, the photos afterward were all gratis, and it was great publicity for each of us chosen to appear in print, but still.

It sunk in that I was going to earn by the hour. Light

dawned. I'm a photo model! What is my rate? What do I charge? I quickly called a commercial print model friend of mine with A+ Agency when I got home that evening. No, dear ones, we did not have cell phones.

"Beginning models are $35 dollars per hour," she informed me.

I thought, "Wow, that would probably be the same amount I made for a show *and* a fitting."

Mr. Heilbron did not look like the romanticized good-look-ing fashion photographer in Michelangelo Antonioni's film *Blow-Up*; he resembled a guy that could be running the hard-ware store in my hometown.

The next day, Friday, I called him. "Hi, Mr. Heilbron, I'm Helen Martin. You said I should call you."

"Yes, Helen, can you work next Wednesday at 1:00 pm? I have a shoot for Field's, but we'll start here." After which he gave me his address.

Wednesday—I had five days to prepare. I packed and repacked my model's bag all weekend. I knew exactly what I needed for a photo shoot, but did not want to forget anything.

At the last minute, I included a 100-watt bulb; we were taught at Patricia Stevens to carry it because you never knew where or what accommodations you would be asked to dress and change in for your job. Whether you posed on the street, the beach, or a restaurant or a vast hotel lobby, next to mag-nificent architecture—the Art Institute of Chicago or the cav-ernous Chicago Library—the many natural settings at Lincoln

Park, Buckingham Fountain or in front of a pub in an alley in Old Town (and these were just a fraction of the great locations where we shot in Chicago (a city to boast about!) the most important thing before you set foot on any of those locations: good lighting for makeup and hair. Hence the light bulb.

I arrived at his studio by cab, of course. I never owned a car in Chicago. One does not need a car since there is a cab on almost every corner or a bus arriving every few minutes, as well as excellent train service. Chicago is the wonderful world of hailing taxis and public transportation. And then I moved to Dallas, and all that went away, but that's another story.

I arrived at his home; really, he did not have a studio. He worked out of doors or on location. Lo and behold, when he sent me downstairs to my dressing room with my first outfit—a two-piece knit—I discovered that the dressing room was a small bathroom with one dim light hanging over the mirror.

My first paid professional fashion shoot, and I had to use my own light bulb for some strong, decent light! That was the only time I carried a light bulb—how boring and what a hassle to carry glass around in your model's bag. In any case, I would have had to purchase another one—I forgot to remove my bulb from the tiny bathroom. But when I came back for another shoot, my 100-watt bulb was there, and the dim one was gone.

Mr. Heilbron later snagged a big campaign, and I was to become part of it.

Throughout the following season, he booked me for a promotion on knit separates. Generally, three styles were shot, and they appeared in the newspaper as three separate portraits displayed below the fold. All of them were photographed on location, stark and stylized with interesting, graphic backgrounds.

Mr. Heilbron was reserved and formal in his interactions. I found out much later that he taught photography at the Chicago Art Institute and some of his work is archived there as well as at the Fashion Institute of Technology in Manhattan.

One day, he informed me we would be shooting at the Ambassador East Hotel. We climbed into his car with wardrobe, camera equipment, my model's bag and hair bag stacked on the back seat. On a future shoot, I would change outfits in that back seat when Lincoln Park was our chosen venue.

We arrived at the hotel, walked through the lobby, and entered into the Grand Ballroom. There were rows and rows of straight-back, upholstered, French-style dining chairs lined up. Setting up his camera, he waved me on set.

I started my poses around and over the chairs. He did not really direct me; I moved, he shot film. We shot three outfits against those chairs. The tear sheet that appeared in the newspaper is tucked away in one of my archival boxes. I was very shy, hardly ever initiated a conversation, and small talk was not my forte. He was a man of few words, so we got along very well.

We unloaded back at the house, and while I was waiting for my cab, he paid my model's fee. Two-and-one-half hours at $35 an hour. Those photographs were instrumental in my getting signed with an agency—the A+Agency saw the campaign and asked me to become one of their models.

Thank you Mr. Heilbron, may you rest in peace.

Print

To become "one of Victor's" was the goal of every fashion print model in Chicago. I was already a successful runway mannequin—booking commercial and fashion print regularly and working in Chicago as well as New York for over a year—but I was waiting to noticed by Victor Skrebneski.

Fashion print modeling and runway modeling are two different disciplines. Runway modeling is all about the walk! In print you must know how to work with the photographer in getting to the "perfect shot"—understanding what the photographer sees through the lens. The model sees herself, her body filling the frame, showing the garment in its best light, all the while mentally framing herself as an artist would to achieve a perfectly balanced canvas.

I waited patiently for Victor to one day see my work and ask me to come in for a meeting. Finally, that day came when Vivian, my booker at A+ Agency, called to say Victor wanted to test me—to see how I appeared and moved on camera. This was during the 1960s. The reigning style was pale skin, pale mouth, tons of kohl eyeliner, and long black eyelashes.

And that is exactly how I looked walking into Victor's studio on LaSalle Street. As a working model, I wanted to be camera ready. I was greeted at the front desk by his booker, Jovanna, always the consummate professional, a fierce and loyal keeper to the Gate of Skrebneski, her reputation was known throughout the industry—one mistake and a model could be banished forever. A force to be reckoned with.

Following behind her, my heart in my throat, I was guided to the make-up room. Victor appeared a short time later, punctual to the minute; woe to the model who was even five minutes late. He looked me over and said, "Hi, thanks for coming." I'm sure I mumbled something back. Victor was every woman's dream—handsome, smart, funny, and charming—and every one of his models managed to fall madly in love with him. I was no exception. I was smitten the moment he touched my face.

With kind words and a million-dollar smile, he picked up a cosmetic sponge and started peeling away my make-up, talking to me all the while, removing a little here, a little there until I had a fully scrubbed face, sans my false eyelashes.

Now it was my turn. I opened my make-up bag and started all over while he looked on, suggesting shadow application for eyelids, contour for cheekbones, and yes, eyelashes were reapplied. He indicated the garment I would be wearing, and smiling, he said, "I'll see you on set." He was gone.

My test outfit was a Marshall Field sleeveless spring collection dress. And then I was finally in front of Victor

Skrebneski and his camera. He shot one roll of film, and when the shoot was over, he thanked me and said, "See Jovanna on your way out."

Back in the dressing room, I packed my bag and changed into my street clothes. I had no idea if I made the cut.

Jovanna's eyes were twinkling and a half smile appeared as I stopped at her desk to thank her. "Call your agent, you have a booking with Victor tomorrow."

My agent had a big smile on her face when I walked into A+ on Oak Street with my book in hand. I entered the "be there" time, tucked it back into my bag, and, walking out to the side walk, an angel gathered me up and carried me to the curb where I hailed a cab. And so began the chapter in my career as one of Victor's models.

An accomplished photographer like Victor is an expert stylist in all things fashion. As I started working for him, I learned he would not "do" my make-up or my hair, but would direct me if I was having trouble getting the look he wanted.

It was also the era of hairpieces and hair attachments. If a photographer wanted bangs for a look—poof, out came the attachable bangs. If shorter hair was wanted, out came a wig. I absolutely had three or four short wigs: blond, braids, lacquered curls, and a variety of "falls," as we called hair extensions.

I loved Victor for many reasons, and trust was one of them. I never had to worry that a potentially unflattering portrait would be shown to a client. He was one of the first fashion photographers in Chicago to dictate what the client would review from a shoot. Some fashion photographers I worked with shot as many as three, four, or five rolls and sent the whole set off to clients. Not Victor. He edited the shoot, showing only the best of the best for clients to select. Victor was known for seldom producing any "bad" shots because of the way he worked— because of his understanding of balance, design, and concept. His unerring eye framed the silhouette in his lens, seeking the correlation of light, shadow, facial expression, the extension and tension of the body, waiting for that second of perfection before he would commit to a take and press the button.

No stylist. No assistant. Just a plain paper backdrop and a stand-alone light. Victor adjusted the light as the model moved, creating a new pose with a tiny turn of her head or making a deeper angle of her hand on her hip. The process is very much like standing in the center of a huge clock, and every movement to change a pose is as small as the second hand moving around the clock. Once a pose has gone through all the many variations, the model creates a new pose, with directions from the photographer, and the process starts again.

Thank you, Patricia Stevens Modeling and Finishing School. I would have fainted dead on the floor if I had not had that training.

If clients were even allowed to watch one of Victor's shoots, they soon learned to keep their suggestions exactly where they occurred: in their heads. I can't remember if we were shooting an ad for a hair product or a beauty/skin product, but I heard the client, who was sitting off the set behind Victor, say to him while we were in the middle of the shoot: "What would happen if she put her hand on her other hip?" Victor answered without missing a beat: "Then her hand would be on her other hip." No more suggestions were forthcoming.

Victor introduced high fashion black-and-white photography to Chicago, demonstrating to the world that the city could be much more than an excellent commercial print town; it could also be a mecca of fashion elegance, transforming "nice photos" into stunning works of art. His innovative genius changed the fashion scene forever. Once I was booked with him I worked for him two or three times per week, and more when fall magazines were being produced.

Chicago was a wonderful backdrop to any kind of shoot with its strong architecture: old-style, magnificent structures dating from the 1800s and 1900s—bold buildings of stone and brick, along with modern glass and steel towers, rising from the Chicago River to meet skyscrapers along Michigan Avenue. The Chicago Art Institute offered a distinguished backdrop with its two giant lions holding court at the entrance. I remember so well posing among Alberto Giacometti's huge black sculptures during the artist's exhibition at the museum. We had Chicago's famous lakefront, expansive parks, fountains, and stunning bridges. Wherever you turned in Chicago, a new venue was waiting for you.

One of my biggest accomplishments in the print portion of my career was the nude photo shoot I was asked to do for him. The "word on the street" was that the world-renowned photographer, Victor Skrebneski, was compiling a book of nudes in black and white. He, of course, was known throughout the industry as one of the top fashion photographers; I was keeping my fingers double-crossed.

The call came from my agency. "Victor wants you to shoot for his book," Vivian informed me.

"Be at the studio 2:00 p.m. Wednesday."

Excited and nervous, I arrived with full make-up. Victor tells me the first shot will be a single; we begin working on my hair—he wants mounds of hair. I open my model's bag, pulling out my falls and hairpieces; we start building the hair high on my head. The long pieces are placed strategically, to cascade down my back like a waterfall. Done.

I have my panties on under my model's smock and head for the set. This would be my first nude shot, and as it turned out, the two shots I do for Victor will be the only nudes of my career. There was never a need to repeat it.

I don't remember being nervous about shooting in the nude as I walked the short walk down the hall to the set. Although, I did have one nudging twinge about agreeing to the shoot because I was worried, of course, about what my mother would say when she saw the photos. I tried not to think about my mother's reaction as I dropped my robe and panties on the side of the set. The only thing Victor and I talked about prior to the shoot was that it would be a standing shot but not frontal.

Standing alone, for my single photo, in front of a white paper backdrop, wearing only what seemed like a million hair pieces and falls cascading down my back, Victor motioned me to turn to the side; I started my first pose, and less than fifteen minutes later, we were finished. He knows how the picture will look before he takes the first frame. He has already created the outcome before you step on set.

In a couple of days, Victor called the agency to ask me to come by to see the shot he had chosen. It is an amazing portrait; the strong curve of my back, the light and the shadows falling along my body line, the subtlety of a breast showing under my arm—and I particularly like that my hand, embracing my waist, forms a perfect line from the tip of my nose to my arm, joined perfectly at the wrist. The portrait that appears in his debut book, *Skrebneski: The Human Form*, is cropped at the lower hip. The original shot he showed me was of a full-length nude. And then it hit me—my mother—I tore my eyes away, looked at him, and said, "Victor, I can't."

"I sorta figured you would say that, that's why I brought you in."

Placing a sheet of paper across my exposed bottom, he started moving it around to find a place to crop where the balance and integrity of the piece would not be compromised, and where I could accept my sainted mother gazing at her daughter in the buff. He stayed with it till he was satisfied with the crop and assured me he was happy with the results. It goes without saying—he could have cut the shot entirely from the book. But that would be so unlike him. Thank you, Victor. The book is extraordinary. A classic in the world of black-and-white photography.

I appear in two shots of this legendary photographer's The Human Form—the single photo and one more, a triple portrait with two other stunning models. The triple reminds me of a Michelangelo marble sculpture.

Giants like Victor nurtured me, helped me to grow, believed in my ability, my professionalism—enabling me to transcend from "okay, she's good" to becoming radiant on set.

Never taking a booking for granted, I always considered it a privilege working with the best talent: photographers, make-up artists, hairstylists, wardrobe stylists, and set designers—each artists at the top of their field. Each call from the agency, every job booked, a gift.

Photograph by Victor Skrebneski

Africa Lost

Uganda 1964. I am with two boys, members of our safari team, sitting in a Land Rover in the middle of the bush. I am sick with fear. We only possess one weapon, and I am holding it. Earlier in the day, I had taken down a game animal for camp food, so fresh meat is stored behind us in the back of the open Rover. My husband Jim and the guide took off through the bush to track Cape buffalo, abandoning me. Selsio, my brave hero, is beside me, who found one of my contact lenses that I had dropped in the tall grass, with young Phillip in the front. The head tracker is gone; the driver is gone; my partner is gone; the guide is gone. I guess I am in charge, and I am terrified.

I hear the lion roar during the first hour, and therein lies the fear. I go over the scenario a dozen times in my head: Selsio will know if the lion is close and spot him in the bush long before I would. If that happens, I will fire a warning shot in the air. That might be enough to make the lion reconsider. But what if he sneaks up behind us? The smell of the meat . . . *dear God, do not give me the task of trying to take a lion down as he rushes the Land Rover.*

I have to smile as Selsio is trying to teach Phillip how to use binoculars. Phillip, so shy and sweet, listens while Selsio, his elder, patiently adjusts the focus, demonstrating the procedure with his hands: the smaller circle, then the larger circle one more time. Phillip continues to nod his head in understanding. Selsio, not so sure, finally plops back in his seat to continue surveying the area.

The boys seem calm. They have seen me in target practice; I never miss. I never wavered when I brought down a Cape buffalo. I took him seconds after he spotted me with no time to find a rest—a small tree, anything to hold my rifle against. I immediately knelt down on one knee, steadied my rifle as I had practiced a dozens of times, and placed my shot. I know my guide was apprehensive. A Cape had seriously injured him.

The sun is slowly arching toward the horizon. Was it just this morning we nodded as we passed villagers who had set up camp beside ours? To field-dress and dry the meat, the women carefully placed the strips on wooden racks they had assembled. They pointed at me and smiled. I wish I were with them now.

The cry of a vulture startles me. They are an unwelcome but persistent presence when we hunt. Fear gnaws at my stomach. Sweating, I'm afraid if I take a drink of water, I will launch into the throes of a vomiting spree. All I want is to be back in London, where we spent a week of sightseeing before boarding the BOAC flight to Benghazi on our way to Entebbe Airport.

Lybia before Gaddafi. Uganda before Idi Amin, when

there was a sense of order. A king still ruled in Lybia in 1964, and Obote in Uganda. Uganda has never fully recovered from Idi Amin's brutal rule. I have often wondered if Selsio, tall, handsome, and very smart, but not of Amin's Kakwa tribe, was killed, as opposition tribes were ruthlessly crushed. As I sat on guard with these beautiful boys, I thought of all the Ugandans we had met in the past weeks—kind, generous, and quick to smile. Never was I wary of my African hosts, and when I was on my own, alone, shopping, having a coffee or tea in a village, I felt at peace and serene.

Africa—we had planned this trip for months. My husband and hunting partner, a veteran hunter, introduced me to the out-of-doors very early in our relationship; in fact, on our second date he took me to a shooting range. He would plan one or two big trips a year—from the Wind River Range in Wyoming to the Yukon to Indonesia or Baja Mexico. But always Africa was in his thoughts for me because he truly knew it would be the trip of a lifetime. For the hunter and world traveler, an African Safari has always been the ultimate, the dreamed-of destination, an exotic land filled with adventure, beauty, and danger. I wanted so badly to feel and live all those elements and to be part of their secret, mysterious world. Yet, suddenly, I am here, deep in the wilds of Uganda preparing to face down a charging lion. Much, much more than any "dream" I held of Africa, more than I had bargained for as a trained hunter, yes, but also as a city dweller who made her living posing for the camera or walking a runway.

Although I eagerly picked up a rifle and learned to hunt, and although I often was the only woman traveling with a group of hunters, I was more accustomed to the ritual of a camera stalking me across a studio, not a life-or-death scenario that depended on my ability to stand fast against a predator who was charging for the attack.

As time passes and we're still "safe," I continue to worry, but somehow the initial stomach-wrenching fear dissipates as we wait for the manly men to return.

I learned early that my training would be extensive if I were to take up a rifle; it would require hours of practice devoted to handling firearms safely. And I was to learn when stalking or tracking that you must "see the animal," not "think" you see it through the brush or trees, and when the choice is made to take the animal—make it a true shot. Injuring and losing an animal is not an option.

We spent weekends hiking and practicing at the shooting range. Hunting became part of our world travels. We immersed ourselves in the cultures, the day-to-day lifestyles of each country, city, and village, from the jungles of the Maluku islands in Indonesia to the mountains of Spain's Pyrenees range. Hundreds of islands form the Maluku chain, some uninhabited. On one of those uninhabited, remote islands, I exchanged bracelets with a young girl working in a field. We were on an expedition as part of an Australian team, at the invitation of the Chief to search his island for a certain horned species that had not been sighted for many years. We were told it had been sixty years since Westerners the likes of us had visited the island. It was thrilling to be greeted by the Chief and his entourage as our little boat pulled up onto shore.

My meeting with the young girl happened on one of the first days of our visit. As we were coming out of the jungle into the outskirts of the village, I noticed a girl of ten or eleven walking through the fields of harvested spices—cloves and nutmeg spread out for drying in the sun. When she approached the village boundary, I met her, and we exchanged greetings, smiling and gesturing as best we could. When she saw a small brass bracelet on my wrist, she touched it gently, running her fingers around it, and then she showed me her beaded one, which I admired. After a moment, and with her face beaming, she indicated we should exchange bracelets. I will never forget her. I have met so many unforgettable people from around the world and am forever grateful to the remarkable strangers for their generosity and gifts of kindness.

Often these gifts came in the form of knowledge—new, valuable life lessons and skills. I learned the proper way to traverse the wild mountains of the Wind River Range of Wyoming. Tall and gangly, Dick Titterington, a legend in the Bighorn country, showed me how to conserve my strength by moving with small deliberate steps, negotiating a rocky mountainside like a skier traversing a snow mountain. Later, I learned to use a walking stick in the gentler mountains of Spain's Pyrenees from a gentleman who joined us as we passed through his small village. Afterward, he presented me with my own walking stick. It stands today in a place of honor by the fireplace. The most intriguing part of our travels was always the discovery: discovering cultures new to us, feeling a closeness with people who live so differently than us, expanding our minds and spirits, and becoming part of the world community.

But this scenario, this lion, this place, my position, where I feel so threatened is not what I signed up for; I was angry, thinking of my dear husband with exasperation. I have been frightened before—it's true—but not like this. I will never forget the first time I heard hunting lions roar in the middle of the night as I laid in my bunk bed with my hand on my rifle beside me, the difference being that Jim was in the bunk next to me. It's an unmistakable sound that no one has to identify for you. It's bone chilling.

I have no interest in hunting a lion or in "bagging" one. I prefer to take game animals that will nourish my friends, my family, and me—nourish these two young villagers, as we become part of their lives, all the while performing the ancient rituals just like the first humans: tracking and stalking, leading up to the moment the decision is made to take the animal. Carefully dressing the meat, arriving back in camp, and placing the meat onto the fire while we gather ourselves together—some of us silent, some talking quietly, but always paying tribute as we honor the animal—we share this food when the bush is quiet. The circle of life completes itself.

Glancing at Selsio and Phillip, who are in Western-style

shorts and shirts, and working hard to keep my mind occupied, I wonder if when they visit their villages, they change into their tribal dress for the duration of their stay. A young man, whom we would befriend, that worked in one of the embassy offices in Nairobi invited us to his apartment and showed us pictures of his mother and father from his village. He was proud when he said, "Of course, when I visit my family, I will change into my native costume."

Dusk is starting to envelope us. Flashlight—check. Uneasily my mind wanders back to a couple of days ago just at dawn as we witnessed a Thomson's gazelle outrun a pack of wild dogs. Dogs have been clocked at 55 miles per hour, yet the gazelle was stronger and faster that day. Wild dogs generally hunt at dawn and dusk, relying on sight rather than smell. At least we have that going for my African friends and me. If a pack spotted us, they would generally keep moving, watching out for stand-up prey.

Sunsets are extraordinary in the African veldt because you can see for miles over the savannah. Animals silhouetted against the sky is an unforgettable sight every time—giraffes, elephants, and kudu marching across the land—but not here in the middle of the bush, thick with brush, grass, and trees.

Wait, what's that? Selsio is sitting straight up, staring into the bush to our right; Phillip's sweet face is anxious as he looks to Selsio for reassurance. I force my eyes to see though the brush, focusing on any small detail that looks out of place: part of a leg, a small movement of a tail, a sloping back; he was looking directly at me when I found his eyes.

My insides turned to water. Without a sound I reached for my rifle, never taking my eyes from him. I could feel Selsio looking at me; slowly I raised my .270 and pointed it to the sky, releasing the safety at the same time. He moved ever so slightly, a ripple of shadow really; I shouldered my rifle and fired my first shot in the air. Reloading I quickly pulled off another one. No movement, no sign. I reloaded for my third and final shot. A distress signal for the hunters as well. I quickly reloaded once again but did not engage the safety. I had one round left in my magazine. Selsio touched my arm and signaled our lion had turned, moving back into the bush. A few seconds later we heard the sound of rifle fire in the distance, three consecutive shots. The men can't be far away.

Selsio was tracking the thick underbrush with his eyes, motioning me to keep my eyes looking in the area where we first spotted the lion. He had retrieved his binoculars from Phillip and proceeded to search the perimeter. Still not one of us had spoken a word.

So the wait starts again, and the fear comes back twofold.

So many times I thought about just starting that vehicle and driving the hell out of there, but I knew I couldn't. "Basic rule of the outdoors, Helen. Never leave your position." Roger that, Jim!

Phillip has finally relaxed enough to look at me, and I give him a small smile. I turn to search the bush again. We hear the men, stepping into the clearing, anxious looks all around as they trot toward us. I wave and smile, to reassure them we are okay. Phillip has a big smile, and Selsio, always the young warrior, remains reserved as he exits the rover to meet his boss and explain the situation. Jim opens my door and asks, "Are you alright, baby?" He always says that; if there were a contest for World Charmer of All-Time he would win hands down. I move into his arms and give him a mighty hug. "A lion, a male lion was right there."

"So you took care of it," he says.

"Yeah, I guess I did," I reply.

I know he has total confidence in how I handle firearms, but to leave me alone in the African bush guarding a fresh kill . . . *think about it dear Jim.*

With rifle still in hand, the initial fear has all but disappeared. I made it; we made it. The three of us survived the awful thing that terrified me so—that I may have had to face a charging animal in the wild. The nighttime nightmares of my childhood had manifested themselves in this place with these two boys. Since I can first remember, of all the predators in the wild, the lion was always the one that signaled the greatest danger to me. I was responsible for myself and two other lives, and I earned the sense of accomplishment that comes from that. The crisis never happened, yet slowly many other emotions surface: relief, exhilaration, and a small bit of disappointment that I was not tested, that I would never know how I would have performed in an all-out lion charge. But when one thinks about it, in the end, isn't it enough to just be prepared? I had prepared mentally and physically for the worst-case scenario. And I succeeded, in that I never showed or revealed what turmoil was going on inside me to the boys, staying calm and smiling at some of their antics, never transferring my fear to them. I am grateful, still, for that one small act of courage.

The big brave men were back—empty-handed I might add—and immediately started asking for things. "Are there any sandwiches around?" I just smiled sweetly as the guide started rummaging around in the kit bag.

The Capes outsmarted them. Having to return before dark settled, I'm sure they were thinking of the night Cape buffalo tracked us back to camp. A small group of two or three was quietly stepping, following in our trail. Darkness soon enveloped us. I was walking smack up behind Jim, my left hand wrapped around his belt, my right keeping my rifle strap steady on my shoulder. Our guide motioned for us to halt and to stand still several times, and we could feel them behind us until, finally, we reached the narrow river where we had felled a tree to traverse it; their stalk was over. We arrived at camp safely, but not before one of our brave trackers fell into the water on his turn to cross the river. He happened to be the one toting the cameras. After much shouting and laughing by all, he made it across, sloshing and scrambling up the bank holding the camera bag high and dry, sporting a huge smile.

Through three decades ending in the 80s, I will travel to Africa many times to seven or eight separate countries, sometimes visiting a country more than once. That Africa is gone, however. My Africa is a memory, locked away in my heart. I have a book in my library called *Vanishing Africa* by Mirella Ricciardi, a melancholy title to say the least. The cover is vivid, showing a young man and woman in full tribal regalia, facing one another, moving to the sound of a rhythmic drum. The innocence and joy of that scene, a scene I witnessed during my travels, will forever be etched in my mind—and so too the lion, my mysterious and elusive lion, who silently appeared, connected with me for a moment and was gone in an instant. Vanished. His all-knowing amber eyes found mine. I feel the answer to the Universe rests in those eyes. Africa is no longer just vanishing; that world, that time, is all gone, lost already.

Hunting
by Moonlight

When my husband Jim and I hunted, there were never any warnings when we came to especially tough stretches, which is probably for the best. The idea is to just keep moving; otherwise, you'll never cross a crevice or a deep ravine if you stop to think about it. The same don't-think-about-it theory applied in Africa. If you worry about stumbling onto a snake, for instance, a Green Mamba or Puff Adder (and we came upon both, as well as cobras), you will never leave your tent.

When mountain climbing, one of the secrets is to never glance down over an edge; the sight of empty space is definitely not what you want, and the sensation can cause you to lose your balance. Night hunting presents similar challenges since you have lost one of your major senses but must forge ahead without fear of falling.

In the early 1980s, Jim and I received word that the Swiss game department had opened up Alpine ibex hunting. Under protection for years, the ibex herds had multiplied and were now threatened by overpopulation. Twenty permits were being offered for 1983 and 1984, and we were thrilled to have two of them. We always loved hunting in the mountains, wherever they may be, especially for Big Horn Rams, and now, we were only the second Americans to be given the opportunity to hunt the Alpine ibex in one of the most beautiful mountain ranges in the world. This was to be my first ibex hunt, and the quest started from a beautiful fourteenth-century castle in the heart of Belgium.

Our travel guide for the four-week journey, Edward Scydlitz, and his wife, Annelien, had leased the Castle Strée-lez-huy and preserved the rooms as they were with the exception of replacing worn furnishings and updating all the bathrooms. We were greeted by the owner, Baron Michel de Moffarts, and learned the castle had been destroyed and rebuilt three times, the last being in 1870. The furnishings were magnificent; it was a showplace of elegant wall paintings with fine bronzes everywhere. The castle's own private chapel completed the awareness of lives lived gracefully long ago. After walking the expansive grounds of the castle and resting for a day, Jim, Edward, and I packed our touring automobile and were off to Switzerland to hunt the Alpine ibex.

We left Belgium and journeyed into the tiny country of Luxembourg and on through part of the Lorraine valley of France, crossing the West German border at Strasbourg. As we came through the Swiss border at Basel, the country started changing to small foothills featuring serene little villages, city squares with perfect church steeples thrusting above the red-roofed houses completing the picture of the charming Alpine landscape. The people we encountered greeted us with smiles and waves.

Seeing the grand soaring Alps for the first time nearly took my breath away. We drove around the edge of beautiful Lake Geneva looking down on villages crowded so closely to its shore they appeared to be tumbling into the water. Nine hours after leaving the castle we arrived in the ancient city of Sion, situated between Gstaad to the north and Zermatt to the south.

We met our guides that evening and were very grateful to have Edward with us since he spoke German and French, two of the three languages spoken in Switzerland, the other being Italian and that one I knew pretty well.

The first morning of the hunt we were up at 4:15 a.m. The day would warm up, but before dawn it was cold. We started with light underwear, several layers of shirts and a sweater, heavy socks and climbing boots—my general North American mountain hunting gear. A jacket over all and with gloves, field glasses, hat, and rifle, we were suited up and ready. At that time, the local guides were usually dressed in the traditional knickers. Handsome and comfortable, knickers, generally seen in that beautiful olive or forest green color we associate with them, are still worn when hiking or climbing in some parts of Europe.

Quite a few years later, I was bird hunting in Scotland and shopped for supplies at the Queen's store, where I purchased several pairs of knickers and long wool socks that came up over the knees to wear under my tall rubber Wellingtons (or "wellies" as Her Majesty refers to them).

We climbed that first morning, stopping every few hundred feet to glass the area. The views were spectacular; photographs, post cards, and movies I had seen of the Alps paled in comparison to new delights every few feet in person. The hardest thing to remember was to concentrate on your footing. All your senses had to be alert.

We saw some ibex on a far mountain range and also some chamois that day, but not an animal we would take. We were looking for older males, past their prime for breeding; experienced guides are invaluable with their knowledge to gauge an animals age, well-being, and condition.

Finally, it was time for lunch. Backpacks were opened and out came a bottle of red wine. I almost fainted straight away. A strict rule we have always adhered to: no drinking during the hunt. I demurred, smiled, and tried very very hard not to appear rude. The wine, perfectly chilled, just happened to come from the game warden's grape vineyard. Being a guest in their country, Jim accepted a small cup from his hand, and "cheers" were said all around. The most wonderful lunch was laid out and served, which included an array of cold meats, sausages, cheese, breads, fresh fruits, chocolates, and pastries of all kinds. A nearby stream provided delicious ice-cold water.

The day we bagged our first ibex was clear and bright and you could see for miles. It happened during the late morning; we spotted ibex high against the skyline across a craggy and what seemed like insurmountable canyon. What a breathtaking and wondrous sight to behold a posed ibex at the top of a high mountain; his recurved horns silhouetted against the sky. We started our climb, splitting up to go down and around, eventually to end up under the animals. The mountain terrain changes considerably while climbing. For a while you are jumping huge rocks, then slipping and sliding on loose small ones, and then again climbing up through small tangles of bushes, but always seeing tiny mountain flowers in bright colors of blue, purple, red, and yellow; wild onions, delicious and sweet.

The last push was straight up, and by this time I had taken off every piece of clothing I could decently remove, binoculars tucked in my shirt, my rifle strapped around me. We kept moving. Jim and I had split up at this point. The chance you take in a stalk like this is that your animals will not be there when you finally arrive within range, since several hours have passed, and you lose sight of them many times during the climb. We had kept well hidden on the last drive and were able to take a well-deserved rest, but not for long. The ibex started to move around; the odds were against success. Besides, we would be shooting straight up at that point, so we waited.

Jim and his guide joined us again, and after a time the ibex started moving, feeding downhill. Then something spooked them, and they all turned and started traversing the cliffs; in a few seconds they would be out of range again. Jim took the first shot, without a rest off his shoulder. Luckily, I was near a small outcrop, so I had a rest; I took my shot immediately after. We each had our Alpine ibex. We were thrilled to have the privilege of hunting the ibex, and being the second American hunters in Switzerland to do so was an added boost.

Since the animals were so high up on the rock cliffs, we had to get them to lower ground to field dress and skin them out. We had plenty of help to carry them down with two men for each animal. Unfortunately, several times during the descent, the animals slipped from their hands and tumbled over sharp rocks; consequently, their coats suffered some damage. Finally we stopped on a small, flat meadow, and Jim started the slow process of skinning the animals; our guides took care of the meat. I started layering up again as the men worked. In about an hour, all the tasks were complete, including wrapping each bundle securely for the decent to the bottom. The horns and skins would go back to Belgium to be dropped off at the taxidermist and made ready for the return trip to the States; included would be entry papers for from the Swiss game department for customs officers in the States.

So many unforgettable moments took place on this trip, but the scenario that garnered laughs every time was the simple act of communication, especially while perched precariously on the side of a mountain, trying to analyze game, to determine the age of the animal, size of horns, distance, wind direction, etc. Many times our game guard would speak French to our guide, which he would translate in Italian to me, and I would then translate in English to Jim. With all this talking and gesturing going on, it is a wonder we saw any game at all!

We arrived back at the game guards' station three hours later to be greeted by a joyful Edward, and, after a hurried conference, we were happily informed that one of the guides would like to prepare a spaghetti dinner for us. So, out of this tiny kitchen, in the middle of the soaring Alps, came the most delicious spaghetti dinner served with tomato and fresh basil sauce, accompanied with good Swiss wine, again from the guards' own winery. We toasted our friendship, our magnificent animals, and the glorious mountains that nurtured them.

We arrived back in Belgium to rest for a couple of days and prepare for our journey to Poland. A day later, the three couples that were to join us on our trip to Poland arrived from the States. So, armed with our precious documents and papers that would get us across East Germany and into Poland, we began the trek that would take me, for the first time, into a country that still had at its helm a communist government.

Edward was our driver once again, so we settled in for our trip northeast across West Germany, past the fashionable city of Cologne with its famous Gothic cathedral, then up to Hanover and onto Helmet where we would spend the night before crossing the heavily guarded East German border the following morning.

The atmosphere was stern and all business. Upon seeing the tall wire fences and the uniformed armed guards in high towers scrutinizing us through their binoculars, the cold, hard realization came to me that I was entering a country where freedom as we knew it did not exist. As I look back on that crossing, I remember feeling utterly helpless and actually fearing a guard might arrest me at any moment. The whole experience was so against what I had ever known as a freedom-loving being. At any moment, my very existence could be violently compromised; I realized that in their eyes I was nothing.

At one of the four check points where our documents were examined by a guard, I happened to glance up to see another guard behind a partition. He was observing the behavior of our examiner through a small peephole. Portable mirrors were used to inspect the underside of our vehicles for smuggled items. Finally, after two hours—and they counted each bullet—our guns were sealed in heavy plastic bags, to be unsealed three hours later when we would leave East Germany and cross into Poland. We were anxious to pass the check point and leave the land mines situated between the fences.

As we crossed through the German countryside, our guide pointed out signs scattered throughout the woods. He was kind enough to translate for us: "Anyone found here will be shot." With that lovely thought in mind, we certainly had no desire to leave the road. We traveled mainly through farm-land, hardly seeing people, machinery, or farm animals. It was like stepping back in time fifty years. Everything—the houses, the outer buildings, the farms—looked as if life had slowed to a crawl. The film had stopped rolling; the projector stopped and went silent.

After passing just south of Berlin, the traffic thinned out, and one hour later we reached the opposite border. There again we encountered exceptional scrutiny of guns, bullets, documents, visas, etc. from the East Germans.

Advancing about thirty yards, the process started all over again with the Polish authorities. After two more hours of biting one's lips and maintaining an outward appearance of patient composure, we were on our way with two additional passengers. Our interpreters had been waiting for us on their side, having arrived by train from Warsaw that morning.

During our stay in Poland, we visited the ancient city of Zielona Góra, which was part of Germany before the Second World War. It has a traditional German-style layout with a large shopping area closed off to motor traffic, allowing strolls through the wide plazas and streets. I joined the other shoppers, queuing up at each little store to see just what might be available for purchase. There was a little activity going on in one dress shop with the arrival of some blouses. Limited selection of merchandise was chronic, be it hardware, food stores, or clothing shops. Unfortunately, much of what they did offer was of poor quality. The network of commerce, goods, transportation, and manufacturing plants to support a thriving economy was still struggling.

I would so much like to return to that gracious city now and marvel at the changes that have taken place since Poland joyfully rejoined the rest of the world.

We arrived in our hunting area called Puszcza Rzepińksa in the evening. The terrain is basically flat and filled with heavy, tall, towering trees. A variety of evergreens are found in the dense forests, and in many places huge fern plants extend for miles.

Our party split up at this point. One group was to be housed about twenty miles away in a grand old mansion at the edge of a small village, while Jim and I took up residence in a newly built hunting lodge. We gathered for meals in the game ranger's home. Our only line of communication to our guides was through our interpreter, Adam, an intelligent young man but not a hunter. We had to be content with hand signals out in the field; consequently, conferences in base camp became daily occurrences.

Everyone in camp was happy about our arrival time because there would be a full moon that evening as well as for the next two nights. With the full moon, we could hunt the wild boar. In fact, being a nocturnal animal, the boar can only be hunted by the full moon because of the need for light; accordingly, we were advised to take a nap after dinner and be ready to start out at 11:30 that night.

I can't quite do justice to the sensation of being in the forest at midnight—it was like being present at the beginning of life when the world was made—the moon shining through the trees caused everything around us shimmer and sent out long shadows across open fields. The forest and fields are alive with life at night. A great pleasure comes to you as you walk under the splendor and grandeur of those magnificent trees, all the while coming into the animals' night world. Periodically, our guide would point toward an area, indicating, I assumed, there were animals present. I couldn't make out anything the first couple of hours; then, slowly I started distinguishing dark shapes at long distances. These shadowy shapes became the objects of the chase. Twenty will quickly melt into the landscape before you can get your field glasses adjusted. Being an observer on this hunt wasn't any less exciting than if I had been a shooter.

We were not lucky on the first night, so went back to camp for an hour's nap before the stag and roebuck hunt that would begin at 5:00 that morning. I was too excited to sleep, reliving the sights and sounds of the past several hours. Around 2:30 in the morning, as we were coming around a stand of trees onto a meadow, we heard loud piercing screams cutting into the stillness of the night. A red fox had found his prey, an unsuspecting rabbit. Sharp and acute thoughts filled my mind as I lay on my temporary bed, recalling the primeval beauty of that shimmering forest.

We were out before daylight and immediately spotted a large stag through the mist, but there was no way you could judge horns without light. We were to see red deer just before daylight five days in a row. We were a little early for the rut, but the stags had started bugling, and we heard antlers clashing in the forest several times during our ten-day hunt.

All over Europe, the roaring of the stag signals the opening of the fall hunt. For centuries, humans were stirred and then beckoned by their call, and we were no different. Just as the bugle of the North American elk causes your heart to skip a beat, so too, the roar of the red deer of Poland plays with your senses.

We passed through several villages, every day driving from one hunting area to another. The Poles hunted very traditionally as they had hunted for hundreds of years. The stag hunt started at 4:00 a.m. and was over by 7:00 a.m. The roebuck hunt started around 6:30 a.m., and you finished up around 8:00 a.m., breakfasted on your return to camp, and then napped until lunch at 2:00 p.m. After lunch, perhaps a little reading or some fishing in the stream behind the lodge, possibly another sleep. Between 4:30 and 5:30 p.m. in the afternoon, we were off again for roebuck in the early part of the evening and stag just before dark, arriving back at camp around 9:00 p.m. for dinner. The whole thing kicks off again when the 3:30 a.m. alarm sounds. I had never hunted quite like this in any part of the world.

The final nights of the full moon we did not take a break, but hunted straight through from 11:00 at night until 8:00 in the morning. Once again, for the first two-and-a-half hours of the boar hunt, the shadows of these ghosts of the night world appear and vanish with such regularity that any semblance of a stalk that put us in shooting range eluded us. We had been skirting the fringe of a densely wooded area for about three quarters of a mile when our guide directed us to glass an open area in the woods one thousand yards to our right. Jim and I spotted the now familiar silhouetted form of these phantoms.

The stir of excitement was with us as this one was nearly twice the size of any previously spotted boars. The wind was in our favor, and without any whispered communication, we immediately started a stalk, swinging slightly to our left through the fringes of the forest. Each one of us followed the others' footfalls carefully and quietly, placing each foot in the exact place the man ahead had vacated. After twenty minutes of moving ahead, we were within 200 yards of the trophy boar. Although this is normal shooting range in daylight, it is almost beyond maximum range by the dimmer light of the moon.

However, since it was all open territory between us and the big boar from this point, we could go not further. With his natural alertness, excellent hearing, and keen sense of smell, there was no possibility of narrowing the distance between us without spooking him. After carefully watching him through the glasses, Jim set up the shooting stick to take the shot. At that moment the animal lifted his head and moved out. Jim dropped the stick, stood up, and at the same time, shouldered his rifle. Finding the boar in his gun sights, he took aim. As the roar of his rifle broke the stillness of the night, the shadowy form of the boar dropped out of the bottom of my field glasses. We maintained our positions, continuing to glass the open area where the boar had been moving. With no sign of movement, we took our bearings and carefully proceeded to his last spotted position. Although we later determined the shot was just over 200 yards, it seemed much further as we eased forward probing through the moonlight haze for our trophy. Suddenly, our guide ahead of us turned and shouted, "Congratulations!"

Good fortune was with us, as he was a truly magnificent boar of 400 pounds.

We did not field dress the animal, but instead, our vehicle (a small truck with driver) had waited a few miles away and upon hearing the shot, started the drive toward us—no radios, no cell phones—just trundling across roads and open fields, through gullies, and around trees, and right to us. At camp, several hours were spent dressing the animal. Jim always joined in since he had been hunting his entire life and learned to field dress game animals as a young boy. The meat was cut, wrapped, and distributed among the guides, drivers, and anyone in our party to take home to their families. Needless to say, we enjoyed delectable, delightful dinners of wild boar with plum sauce, served with rice or potatoes. Roast stew became another dish, as well as boar meat sandwiches for our lunches.

I've always loved the roebuck since I first discovered them in Spain and collected a gold medal trophy there. Now, I was thrilled to have the chance to take one in Poland. A very clever animal that has survived in the forests of Europe for centuries, the roebuck's portrait has been captured grandly in the company of royal personages in paintings. Indeed, the roebuck belongs in that lofty company for he carries on his antlered head a magnificent small crown.

I took my roebuck on the eighth day of the hunt in Poland. About 7:00 a.m., we were moving along the edge of the forest—filled with a morning fog—when our guide spotted him as he stepped into a clearing. We immediately dropped out of sight, and I watched him through my glasses about 250 yards away. There are so few places for a gun rest in the forest, and just as I had learned to use the walking stick in the Pyrenees of Spain, I learned to use the shooting stick in Poland.

During the day, I spent time practicing with this tricky device. The two narrow sticks are about five feet long and are joined by a bolt about 4" from the ends. When you are ready, you swing the sticks apart, plant them on the ground, and rest your rifle in the small groove at the top, holding stick and rifle steady at the same time while you pull the rifle butt into your shoulder as you shoot. After I got the go-ahead nod from Steve, our guide, I slid my rifle off my shoulder, adjusted my shooting stick, found the roebuck in my crosshairs, and as he was moving out, I took a deep breath, held it, and squeezed. I had my second European roebuck.

Thousands of miles had been crossed; time, energy, and money had been spent, and it was all worth it at this moment in this forest in this country of Poland.

One of the sights of Poland I remember vividly is the overwhelming beauty of the red stag. We hunted them two ways. One was to listen for their bugle and stalk them through the forest, observing where they had been eating or where they stopped to scrape their antlers on tree limbs. The second way was for the hunter to occupy a high stand at the edge of the forest, entered an hour before dawn, and wait until daybreak, much as they hunt in Texas. We hunted both ways, and about equal time was spent in both situations.

Of course, we were able to see the herds while concealed in a blind. The rewards received from sitting immobile for hours in a blind were monumental. The blinds were very high wooden structures and had to be entered by ladder in total darkness. There were two mornings I remember in particular that the three of us— Jim, myself, and the guide—were especially quiet; no sneezing had occurred, no one had dropped their field glasses or knocked their rifle against the wall.

When daylight came and the heavy fog dissipated, far into the distance shapes and images came into focus. Slowly, as you strained staring through the mist, the images unfolded before your eyes and became beautiful, beautiful red deer. Prancing, stately old gentlemen with heavy thick collars around their necks, past their prime were nonetheless still strutting proudly. Middle-age bucks in their prime—strong, light in color with elegant sweeping antlers—then the younger ones—cocky, sure of themselves. And always the alert and watchful females, especially when they had their young along. We counted between 75 and 100 animals in the two herds.

Jim took his stag on the only day I was not able to make the morning hunt. The 3:30 a.m. calls were gutting me after the all-night hunting marathons. We continued hunting several days for my stag but never found him. My stag is still there waiting.

We left Poland with mixed feelings, sad to leave our new-found Polish friends and the deep, dark mysterious forests.

But considering that this was the 1980s and the Cold War was still in full swing, we were relieved to journey back to countries that were more in tune with the form of democracy we recognized. The Polish people were fighters, and as we departed, I saluted their strength and their love of country and tradition.

The Great Dallas Apparel Mart

Most freelance runway models started out as house models, learning to walk in couture clothes and to move in them easily, wearing them as our own. The experience was invaluable for up-and-coming models. "Mr. Eddie" auditioned me on the second floor of his namesake store, Blum's Vogue, on Michigan Avenue, called the Magnificent Mile in Chicago. The couture floor, where a small runway and stage were used to "show" for private customers, was situated in front of the windows overlooking the Avenue and Lake Michigan beyond. Just like the movies, I thought to myself.

I had never heard of the designer, James Galanos (later, Stanley Marcus would dub him the greatest American designer), but I was handed a gown with a red velvet strapless top and black satin long skirt that fish tailed into a small train. All my training I had received at school came into play. This would be the first time I had ever worn a couture garment; the moment changed my perception of modeling. I was no longer a model but a high fashion model. I floated out in that gown with the straight black satin stole trailing behind me and was hired on the spot. I have always loved fashion, but that event became the seminal point in my life—when I was introduced to couture.

Through all the dozens and dozens of runway fashion shows I have walked, hundreds probably, nothing could prepare me for my first show in the Great Hall at the Apparel Mart in Dallas, Texas. Yes, the same Great Hall where the futuristic *Logan's Run* was filmed in 1976.

Kim Dawson Agency headquarters was on the same floor behind the Great Hall so we saw the actors and film crew during their stay; paying little attention to them, I might add. There was always something going on in that enormous cavern of a space besides runway fashion shows. Some of the agency actors were cast in *Logan's Run*, but the modeling and broadcast divisions were totally separate, so our interest in what was going on outside of ourselves lasted a nanosecond.

The building is gone now, but not the memories. The building, which had been constructed in 1964 by the legendary builder, Trammell Crow, was demolished in 2006. I visited his son, Harlan Crow, in his office at the beautifully renovated old Parkland Hospital building on Oak Lawn. We talked about those brilliant days. I started modeling there in the very early 70s when retail buyers came from across the globe to visit the many dozens of showrooms, placing orders with the vendors for the Spring/Summer, Fall, and Resort seasons. And how sad it was for all of us—models, fashion designers, manufacturers, photographers, set designers, sound and light people, senders, dressers, make-up and hair artists, musicians, agency bookers—how very sad we all were, to see that sprawling building come down: the largest wholesale fashion market in the world under one roof, a world much like Brigadoon that comes alive not once per century but fourteen times a year. Kim Dawson Modeling Agency produced seventy fashion shows annually for the five yearly women's apparel markets, each market lasting five days. I related my feelings to Harlan about driving everyday to KD Studio and passing that huge building, watching each floor disappear, until finally, the era that once housed the world-famous wholesale market closed forever behind a cloud of demolition dust.

We chatted awhile, and then, turning, he pulled a small square stone from a side table and presented the memento to me. The plaque attached to the original stone reads: The Dallas Apparel Mart, with the opening and closing credits displayed. As a young man he had watched the Mart grow, through his father's eyes, to become one of the largest whole-sale venues in the country.

❦

Come with me backstage at the Apparel Mart:

"Helen, you're up!"

Panic . . . can't find my shoes. Elaine borrowed them for her last change; she promised they would be back. Oh, here they are . . .

"Helen, you're on!"

"Wait." Daria, the formidable Neiman Marcus Fashion Director, quietly demands as she pulls me to the accessory table to clasp a cuff on my wrist and hands me a pair of earrings.

Breathe . . .

Behind the curtain, the sender touches my shoulder; I prepare to make another entrance in the Great Hall during market at the Apparel Mart in Dallas.

"Wait, who do I follow?"

Each and every model knows she had better follow the sacred lineup. Kathy Tyner, talent agent, founder, and award winning president of KD Studio, was one of the "keepers" of those lineups. Why is the lineup so important? Because every manufacturer and designer has paid for the model to "walk" his or her garment. Kim Dawson, former model, founder, and president of the famous Kim Dawson Modeling Agency, is narrating each one of the six, seven, or eight pieces I will be modeling during the morning show. Well over one hundred to two hundred garments during a show was a walk in the park . . . and it is my cue—too late!

I am at the top of the stairs; the stairs run across the width of the stage before dropping onto the stage itself. And because no fashion show coordinator can bear to look up and see a bare stage; the stairs are filled with models, situated beautifully on each level. That's what we do: we "situate" ourselves. When a model forgets what she is suppose to do or where to pose in a scene that was rehearsed at dawn, she just falls back on the tried-and-true saying in model talk: "just go where there isn't anybody," and you will never go wrong. Still, I have to remember who I follow before Kim has to say, "Let's look at you, Helen."

Damn it! Too late . . . I'll know who I follow for my next change.

Our beloved Kim! There are so many wonderful stories about her kindness, all-encompassing love, and absolute devotion and loyalty she exhibited for her models, which was legendary, even when we messed up. She had rules for that, such as, "It's only a fashion show, it's over!" Another rule: "No one starts out to do a bad show!"

But watch out! If anyone directly opposed an order she had stated during the pre-show meeting, then we were in for it. Watching her storm back stage, grab a chair to stand on, hands on hips, her voice rising. *Oh, oh, now she's yelling*—we knew we were in for it.

"Can anyone explain to me what a double means? What a triple means? I guess not because some of you only do singles!"

"When the lineup calls for doubles, I want to see two models working together, that means addressing the audience side-by-side. Doubles mean walking and doing your routines together!"

Then she pauses, relenting a bit.

"You all are so good about reading each other's moves that it's wonderful to see doubles and triples working the runway."

Then she is mad again. "And it is soooo boring and it takes up too much time watching one more beautiful model float down the runway in single file!"

Off the chair she would come and storm out.

The legendary Kim Dawson Agency is in full force today, maintaining its place as one of the top agencies worldwide. And at the helm is Lisa Dawson, who continues to carry on her parents' legacy.

Scotland

Scotland

Wyoming

Wyoming

Baja, California

West Texas

I Have to Drive There

Long before there ever existed a GPS app on my phone, the standard mode of operation for me was a piece of paper filled with so-called directions taped to my dashboard, or printed *MapQuest* directions, generally inadequate or sadly outdated. This should be fun, I think, as I scan the flyer advertising dance classes in North Dallas, specifically ballroom dancing taught by a friend of mine—a most charming guy who just happens to be tall, dark, very handsome, and very single.

Heaven knows I need the movement.

As far as exercise goes, running is out, racquetball went the way of my word processor (and I am still sorry to this day that I got rid of it, but I was told, "Now you have to have a computer, and you can do so much more with it," etc. etc. mumbo jumbo, la tee da), and also tennis is out, trail hiking, and skiing. Let's see, when was the last time I strapped those leg breakers on? That was more than twenty years ago.

What activities are left now for my creaky joints: walking, yoga, working out with weights. Don't—do not laugh. I lift eight pound weights straight up to shoulder press, and I hook up on weight machines pushing 30 to 35 lbs. You're not laughing now are you?

So, why can I not go to this handsome man's weekly dance classes? Because I have to drive there.

For example, the I'm-getting-very-nervous-driving thing begins when I am invited to a show, let's say somewhere in Arlington, a city sandwiched between the freeways of Dallas and Fort Worth. First, my friend gleefully informs me, we'll meet for dinner at the Hot Rock Rib and Pulled Pork Emporium on Fifth and Main, and then we'll drive to the theatre—it's just five minutes away. Five minutes away by helicopter seems more accurate; by car, in evening traffic, the drive will take about fifteen minutes.

Why do I know these things? Because it always happens; that's just the way things work in these parts. First, you have to contend with the one-way streets, then with the construction, and then, of course, if your friend did not actually give you a street-numbered address, you must assume you will spend several precious moments scanning for the building. A Texan's directions generally go like this: "You can't miss it, it's across from Denny's"—or the new bank building, or a couple of doors down from the fire station, or the donut shop with the pink sign, or the Walmart with endless parking lots, or the "something." Why do Texans do that?

The following directions are the actual instructions to a restaurant that specializes in catfish that I received (I do love catfish so I accepted):

"Keep going on whatever street you can, turn right at the church, then when you come to a Y in the road, take the right and you will cross a railroad. Keep going, and if you see a big silo, you have gone too far, so turn around, and it is just past the railroad track (how long or far is "keep going?"). It's on your right; it sits back off the road, but there is an orange sign with an arrow painted on it." After I had passed the legendary restaurant for the third time, I tried again—this time driving slowly on the shoulder so my headlights could catch the sign. Of course, by the time I was in the correct vicinity, darkness had descended all around me. I was totally disheveled when I arrived and did not even receive a prize for solving the "direction puzzle."

I am originally from Chicago. Chicago is set on a grid just like New York City. Being used to directions such as 3600 North and 1200 West, I am constantly denounced as a coward and declared weak-willed when I refuse to set out on a journey equipped with driving instructions like "you can't miss it" and "don't pay any attention to the numbers." My mode of transportation used to be so civilized; the Leave-the-Driving-To-Us world is gone forever for me. How I miss those buses, the transfers, the trains that were always on time like the mighty "L," and my favorite: cruising cabs on almost every street and corner.

I am not a car person. It started years ago. Shortly after moving to Dallas, I became aware that city elections were coming up soon, which for me meant a trip to the courthouse to register. So, with carefully written instructions taped on my dashboard, and the assurance of a light traffic day, I headed downtown.

I knew things were going too well when I made the twenty minute drive in only forty-five minutes, and finding the court-house was not difficult either; in fact, I knew exactly where it was located since I had driven past it about eleven times trying to find a parking place.

All the same, I was in tears by the time I saw the traffic policeman coming up on my left. His heroic appearance at this moment of crisis was the answer to my prayers; in his hand-some navy uniform covered with police regalia, he became my shining light. Blinded with happiness, I drove straight to him, which immediately forced him to jump out of the way, causing him to lose his balance. As I watched him fall to his knees, the look he gave me would have made the likes of Alexander the Great turn away, but this man represented salvation to me, someone I could talk to about this monster I was chained to. Tears streaming down my face, I jumped out of the car, ran to him, and while pleading forgiveness, I informed him how terribly sorry I was about having to leave my car right where it was since I could not find a parking place, and that it didn't matter what he did with the thing, and if I never saw the car again, it would certainly be all right with me.

He didn't answer but gazed past me looking for help. Spotting a fellow officer on a motorcycle, he motioned him over for a conference.

After a while it was decided the motorcycle officer would

lead me to a safe place. Those few minutes following that brave, wise policeman to my parking place, which he personally chose for me, were the happiest moments I have ever had behind the wheel.

One would think that after many years living and driving in Dallas, things would get easier. No, no, no. The new scourge that is fostered upon unsuspecting drivers in downtown Dallas is urban development in the form of brand new hotels, restaurants, and apartment complexes. These have sprung up by the dozens, obliterating any old landmarks that might have helped me on my journey into the place called You Can't Drive There.

The most recent embarrassing incident happened several years ago when I was invited to join some friends at a new downtown restaurant on Harwood. H A R W O O D. I have seen signs reading Harwood, of course, but I can't remember ever driving to an actual address on Harwood—using the street as a point of reference would have been my only association. And now, it seems, I have to find a brand-spanking-new restaurant on a busy downtown thruway. Right away I know I will not get a street number because I am sure there *are* no street numbers (at least no numbers you can see from the street, where one would be driving).

Additional information I did not receive: Harwood is a one way street. Knowing the side of the street on which the restaurant is located would have helped as well.

Probably, I could have found it if I were coming from the

opposite direction. I can't drive there because I can't get there from here: here would be from Turtle Creek and Cedar Springs, so I keep driving past the Crescent, trying to find it while talking on the phone with my friends already seated in the restaurant and even having an emotional chat with their waitress, whom, I'm sure, is dropped off for work by her boyfriend because she could never find it on her own from the directions she is giving me. I talk with three people while I cruise around the area—my host, his friend, and their waitress—ending up on Maple several times and circling around again to Cedar Springs. These were my instructions during this insanity.

"I can see the Rolex Building from the window," says my host.

I know where the Rolex building is; I just can't drive there.

"How far away is it from the Crescent?" I ask.

"It's just over two blocks," they answer.

"Which way?" I ask. "The Crescent is on my left."

"We can see the Crescent from the patio," they report.

"It's in the St. Anne's new high-rise—the restaurant has torches all around the outside patio, you can't miss it!"

That's it!

I am so out of here. I pull into the Hotel Crescent Court, where the valets all know me—I work out in the Spa—but for a moment they do not recognize me because I am dressed for dinner with eye makeup and am not wearing my sweats. Instead of a sleepy, drowsy, relaxed face greeting them, they are confronted with a wild-eyed, over-dressed blond on the verge of a nervous breakdown.

As my window rolls down, I blurt out, "Where's the St. Anne building restaurant with the torches out front? Can we see the building from here?" I look pleadingly at the hotel chauffeur they have called out front to help me.

He replies, "No, not really."

So, it's decided. I will leave my car, and this brave, wise hotel staff member will drive me. I hop into the hotel car and am chauffeured through several lights, going left since he cannot go right, safely depositing me off on a side street because he could not get on Harwood from here either.

I have passed the restaurant on my right since, as I traveled one-way on Harwood, and upon seeing it for the first time from the front, I decided it doesn't seem right for a restaurant to be on an incline up off the side of the road with the silly torches lining the patio. These new restaurant owners have to locate someplace where I can find them. Ocean Prime comes to mind, as does Al Biernat's and The Mansion. Those are civilized locations where a single, charming, older woman can arrive in a calm, relaxed state, instead of a state of frenzied-white-knuckled-silent-screaming fear.

After remembering these fiascos, I have decided the dance classes will have to wait until someone can drive me there, and since I can see the Crescent from where I live, and driving there is a breeze, I will have to settle for my yoga classes right now. What a shame—another exciting adventure snuffed out because I can't drive there.

¡Viva Hispania!

I have never considered Spain a game-hunting haven like Africa or North America. It's not. It's much more. To me, Spain has always been one of the Romance countries like Italy or France, and I always thought of Madrid as an international setting like Istanbul. One visits these countries and cities to experience the artistic accomplishments in architecture and music and to purchase handcrafted art, or to sun on the seashores, or to gaze at snow-capped mountain ranges from the veranda of an ancient castle. You can do all of this in Spain. You also can have extreme adventures. Besides gazing at mountain ranges, I became a mountain climber, hitting those slopes, crevices, and rock piles head on to experience the age-old ritual of fine game-hunting.

At that time, Alfonso Fabrés and Félix Lalanne ran a safari company called Huntinspain, which the Fabrés family continues to operate today. I hunted with them and Juan Fabrés on two separate occasions. These gentlemen are of the highest order—expert guides who lead you to your quarry as well as to some of the best restaurants in Spain. I can't say enough about Spanish food. Every meal is a delight, from fresh fish on the coast to roast lamb and cabrito with an incredible array of fresh vegetables to bread that you cannot stop eating, and I cannot leave out my favorite Spanish dish, paella.

Madrid became our base camp on those trips, and during one memorable safari, after a day or two of sightseeing, we packed away our city and evening clothes, donned hunting attire, and departed to hunt chamois and Spanish ibex. Our first destination was the Gredos Mountains west of Madrid, in search of the Spanish ibex.

We arrived at a small village near an icy water stream that provided a trout for dinner before retiring. The hunt would begin early the next morning. Really! Hunts always begin very early in the morning—much to my dismay. The only way I could every make it for "ready" time was to lay out absolutely everything the night before. The last thing we women want to do is have the men standing arount waiting for us. Heaven forbid. Although I was not personally going for ibex, I made the hunt with Jim to get some climbing in before going to the Pyrenees.

My first day's hunt was to be the toughest of the entire trip. The Gredos are rough, boys and girls. It's like God built these simple mountain peaks and then decided to throw eight billion rocks on each one. Make that each side of each one. We drove as far as we could, then left our vehicle and started the climb at about 9:00 a.m. Twelve hours later, I would finally get a glimpse of the town below.

It was rainy that morning, and after climbing for an hour,

we started glassing for ibex and saw some across the canyon, but they weren't what we wanted. Several times, we had to stop and find shelter from the rain, once in a sheepherder's stone lean-to. After a while the sky began to clear, and we started up the mountain again. Our last big push was a great rock-strewn stream. Some of the boulders were as big as houses, so we used the famous rock-hopping trick that we had used in the Wind River Range of Wyoming. I could get a nice rhythm going, but I had to be super alert and not break concentration. Needless to say, it was the type of workout that would strike fear in the hearts of even the most fit athletes; somehow my long legs and I accomplished it.

Later that afternoon, we topped out, and though we had an ibex in sight, we couldn't tell the length of his horns, so we left him. Climbing around to the other side, we glassed for a long time up and down the canyons around us, spotting several. It was then that I saw something that I had seen in so many photographs. Behind and high above us, an ibex was perched at the very top of a rock pile, silhouetted against the skyline and looking straight down at us. It was an incredible sight; our guides could tell he was still valuable to the herd, not past his prime, so we did not pursue. On the long climb back down the mountain, we attempted to get a better look at the game we spotted that morning; after glassing and enjoying their presence, we headed back.

It was growing dark as we completed our descent. I could see the town below, and the thought of food and drink gave me the last push I needed to make it in. I was totally exhausted, but it had been a truly exciting day. Hunting involves great effort; tracking an animal, hours of walking, climbing—but being outdoors enriches the soul, so the hunter revels in the beauty of nature, accepting any day in the field as a reward.

I let Jim and Alfonso climb the mountain without me the next day and went on a sightseeing tour with our friends, the Fritzes. We toured a breathtaking cavern, which was discovered in 1963 by two boys who happened upon it while playing. Naturally, we were hungry after our excursion and had a delightful lunch of red deer stew. We dined in a Parador, a rejuvenated castle, built in the thirteenth century, located in the province of Toledo. The architecture of the castle reflected the eight centuries of the Moorish occupation of Spain. Then we stopped in a small town called Oropesa to buy linens. The embroidery is done locally and is quite beautiful.

Jim was successful in getting an exceptional ibex that day. It was in the silver medal class, so we set out for the Pyrenees bright and early the next morning, stopping for a while in Madrid. We traveled through Guadalajara with an overnight stay in Castillo de los Obispos, originally a Roman castle, later occupied by the Moors. This Parador was built in 1124, and we slept very well in our royal rooms. The next day, we visited the Lalanne family winery. Needless to say, we had to do some wine tasting—ah, quite a bit of wine tasting. Later in the day, we made a tour of the beautiful cathedral in Zaragoza with a stop at Castillo de Loarre in Huesca.

Huesca is high in the Pyrenees and not far from the French border; in fact, during our days in the mountains, we could see the French Pyrenees. This mountain village is charming, picture-postcard perfect. Winding streets lined by two- and three-story homes connect at the main plaza. There, we found several restaurants and little shops loaded with mountain climbing gear and skiing equipment.

It was in these mountains that I learned to use the walking stick. I got tangled up with it a few times and fell flat. I can do that without a stick, too, but eventually I managed to get the hang of it. I used my walking stick to jump over crevices, rushing brooks, and small streams. There were times when crawling up on my hands and knees seemed a better idea.

The Pyrenees are incredibly beautiful. We hiked up the side of the mountain under stately evergreens, crossing a glacier or two, breathing in the fresh air, and admiring the alpine flowers.

The ranges are so vast that the shots you have to take are long. Alfonso spotted a good chamois across a canyon late in the morning. I couldn't see him until I picked up my scope. It seemed silly to continue glassing when they were so far away, so we gave up and went on. Early in the afternoon, we spooked another, then stumbled and climbed and huffed and puffed our way after him. Those little guys are really fast, and he was long gone. Since the day was rapidly warming we took a break and peeled off a few layers of clothing.

Finally, toward the end of the day, the guides spotted three bucks grazing on the ridge below us. They were unaware of our presence. After much signaling and glassing, I eventually determined which one I should take. The chamois must have picked up our scent because they began to move around. "It's now or never," I thought to myself. Before they could move on, I got off a shot and brought down a very nice one.

We stayed in the village several days to finish the hunt and then headed north, traveling through Basque country, across the top of Spain close to the coast. After nine hours of driving, we arrived in the Cantabria area north of León to hunt roebuck.

The regal roebuck is an elusive animal and must be hunted in the early morning and late evening hours. You're up at 5:00 a.m. and in place before sunrise. If nothing happens, it's back to town for lunch and a siesta, then out again about 4:00 p.m.

It is a waiting game for this animal. We performed the standard ritual for several days, and then one afternoon as we were seated in a grove of trees looking out across a flat grassy area, a roebuck moved out from behind a row of low-lying bushes. I could see him periodically as he moved in and out of the cover. There was no need to ask if he was a good one. One glance at Alfonso, and I knew. I used a stick for my rest and took careful aim. My shot proved true. He was a magnificent trophy, my first gold medal game animal from Spain. I was thrilled beyond words.

We stayed on until Jim could collect his roebuck. Since mine was a gold medal, the pressure was on. I assured him that there is a great deal of luck to trophy hunting, and I simply happened to be in the right place at the right time. It could just as easily have been him. I didn't bother to add that I am the better hunter.

For fallow deer hunting, we went south from Madrid through Ciudad Real, Don Quixote country, and hunted on a ranch owned by one of Spain's most famous bullfighters, Don Luis Miguel Dominguín, now deceased. The ranch is located in high mountain country but is surprisingly easy to get around in. Within the boundaries of the property, perched high on a cliff is a lovely monastery and chapel called Virgen de la Cabeza.

The highlight of the fallow deer hunt was the dinner given in my honor by the guides and local residents. It was held in a tiny building, just one room with a fireplace. Still in our hunting clothes, we dined on baked chicken, rice, and good wine. After dinner, I was introduced to Flamenco dancing. We had seen famous dancers in Madrid, enchanting men and women of such style and grace they take your breath away. I had never thought to try it myself, but it looked so exciting. As I watched, I was told that most of the best Flamenco dancers in Spain come from this area, and I could see why. Everyone dances or sings and plays the guitar. Children of all ages learn the steps and the rhythmic clapping from their parents. Entire families dance. Traditional songs are handed down from one generation to the next. We danced and drank wine, then danced and drank some more wine. I tried to capture the rhythm, failing most of the time, but when I did catch it, even for a moment, I was thrilled. I will never forget the warmth and love shown us that evening.

From the Domínguín ranch, we went to the Beceite Mountains off the northeastern coast to hunt mouflon sheep. Our Parador was situated on a hill overlooking the town of Tortosa and the River Ebro. We could see the old city wall from the ramparts of our castle.

Wake up call was at 5:00 a.m., and after a quick orange juice, we drove to a little village to pick up our local rangers. We went by Land Rover through the foothills, then left our vehicle at the end of the trail and traversed up the mountains on foot. It was extremely windy that morning. The wind literally knocked us off our feet, forcing us to find shelter in a grove of trees. We broke early for lunch and started out again, but the wind was still fierce, and we settled in for a nap to wait it out.

Early afternoon found us climbing steadily, traversing, circling, glassing the mountains, just as we had done on our bighorn sheep hunts in Canada. We could see the Mediterranean Sea at certain points during our climb. On our way, we spooked a ram, but Jim couldn't get set fast enough to fire off a shot.

We stopped, glassed again, moved on to the next ridge and spotted some sheep feeding way below us. We waited for them to slowly make their way up the mountain. The pause gave me an opportunity to take a nap.

Suddenly, I heard this commotion. Juan had spotted the big one and orders came instantly; pick up gear, keep down, move out. We duck-walked and crawled our way up and around so Jim could get a good rest. Throwing his coat over a rock, he placed his rifle over it and positioned himself for the shot. It was to be a long one, but it was accurate. The ram was in the gold medal class. It was a fine way to end our hunting adventures in Spain.

Thinking back on Spain, the name conjures up spectacular images of ancient walled cities and of the people who passed their lives there, of children's shining faces as they dance the old way, of fashionable homes and the broad boulevards of Valencia. Into focus come memories of my beautiful roebuck, and the happiness of the local guide when I snagged my fallow deer. After all, I was just a woman. I have vivid images of the day I met the ibex at the top of his world. But the thing I remember the most about Spain, the memory and the image that appears most often in my mind, is the one of good friends seated around a table enjoying companionship, sharing food we brought in from the fields and mountains, enjoying laughter and fun while exchanging campfire stories.

The Body Changer

I'm a writer, and being a writer is all about rewriting—first, second, third drafts—reconfiguring the timeline, throwing pieces of text out, replacing them (out of thin air, I might add) with something else, reconstructing and refitting the pieces; inserting, perfectly, each piece of the puzzle, in other words, revision-hell; editing, restyling the format, doing leg-work, and spending time on researching background material.

That same dread, doubt, frustration, vexation, wishing-to-be-some-place-else experience occurred during my fittings and refittings for a gown I purchased not too long ago.

Never, never order a knit sheath gown if you are over twenty-two years of age, even if you have the top expert seamstress/alteration professional at the downtown Neiman Marcus at your disposal. Attention: an unlined knit, floor-length St John's gown has no place to go except to follow the lines of the body it falls over!

Gosh, it looked so beautiful in the photo: jeweled neck-line, long narrow sleeves, tight at the wrist, covering the model's hand just to the tops of the fingers. I love a statement sleeve—Snow White and all the mythical princesses wear that sleeve. Waistline defined, cut low in the back, the gown falling to the floor, allowing a smooth flow and movement as one walks, created for a model's figure. I wanted that look again, my model's look once more.

But alas, I had forgotten about the dreaded Body Changer—the monster that stalks women of a certain age, moving our body parts around at will, sideways, back and forth, up and down at the same time, raising my upper hip line into my waist area and rearranging what once was a smooth lower back into perfectly placed pleats.

My body line is the same: long legs, narrow hips; my bottom is still nice, but now I'm suddenly short waisted, have a tummy for all to see, AND I chose a fitted knit dress. As Jay Leno said to Hugh Grant when he was caught in a compromising position, or as he might have asked the princely Prince Harry when he chucked his knickers, "What were you thinking?"

I look great in my clothes because I understand the concept of balance and design, and I am a master at the art of camouflage.

But there would be no stoles, no wraps, no asymmetrical dropped belts; this time, I had nothing. I was on my own, there was nothing else to do except to shift into serious battle mode.

So, into the closet to pull out every Spanx in every size that I had ever purchased and never worn; I have small, medium and large in most styles; padded bras, no-pad bras; waist cinch corsets with bones and without; high-waist Spanx that came to just below the bra—when did I buy that thing? Keep in mind, the garment cannot flatten my bottom. Do I even have a merry widow, or did I get rid of that beauty? I pulled out all sorts of body suits and corsets with long stays in small, medium, and large as well as thong styles, but the edge of the stays poke through the gown in the small of the back and the fit is too loose in the medium and large. So back to the lingerie department for more styles, a variety of styles, on and on. Three fittings later, the perfect piece from Nordstrom. A black satin waist cinch with hidden bones and a separate perfectly fitted bra in a 36 B. By the way, my breasts are still fantastic!

By wearing the cinch, regular sheer panties, and my smooth perfectly fitted bra, I'm thinking: this may work. And as the dress fell over my body, I settled in, posed, peered in the mirror, and the silhouette I wanted appeared; one could see the slight outline of the cinch, which looked like a bustier, and, therefore, part of the dress—another mythical princess look.

Several times, during the worst of times, I was on the phone with my dear friend from Houston: a super chic "Best Dressed Award" recipient, she encouraged me, reminding me to work my perfect posture and model's walk.

Back to the closet: Where are my patent high heels? My most comfortable shoes with a small platform, open toe and sling heel, in the most amazing eggplant color with black heel? Got 'em!

I was back in my fashion model mode. The time: 2:00 p.m. Hair dresser's: 3:00 p.m. My date was coming in from out of town for the event and would be at my house when I returned home at 4:30. My fingernails and toenails had to be painted; I chose a deep, rich red and did the deed at home.

One final check for makeup, and I suddenly thought, oh my gosh, what about earrings? My accessories are displayed within easy reach in my closet/dressing room, so I opened my earring trays, and quickly chose the jet black drop earrings I purchased years ago after a fashion show at Marshall Field's in Chicago. That makes them vintage, i.e. very cool.

We were ready. My date dazzled in his Armani tux with the most amazing white embossed, stripe patterned Italian designer shirt I have ever seen.

"My gosh, my love, how much did that shirt cost you?"

"It's a $600 shirt; I got it on sale for half." Amen.

We looked spectacular; I had accomplished the look I wanted. Helen Martin, when I had walked the catwalks all those glamorous, glimmering years ago. Walking my model's walk into the black-tie dinner event, I felt "new" again. Posture perfect; one has no choice, really, cinched in like that.

Sitting at dinner, I felt so alive and alert. I know my overall visage glowed. All my movements were fluid; rising from my chair, walking over to greet someone at another table, feelings of weightlessness and lightness in my limbs, my happiness knew no bounds.

And just as night follows day, water is wet, and ice is cold— and you did something stupid when the boy you liked in high school made eye contact with you—a model will never stop looking for the camera in the room, planning and calculating to be ready when the photographer walks up to you and your date and says the magic words: "I'd like to take your picture?"

Posing for a photo would be a no-brainer if you were on your own for a single shot, or with a gentleman in the fashion industry because he knows—each should move together, shoulders slightly touching, so you have a feel for how your date will "situate" himself, and at no time will he put his arm around you. If he is super cool and aware of how all this works, take his arm and then you can work the pose while he is being wonderful on his own. I always practice in front of the mirror in my outfit before I go out, so I was ready: weight on one leg, hip out, hand placed beautifully on hip, showing fingers spread, wrist dropped, other arm slightly curved on my body, front side of hand toward camera, space showing between elbow and body, moving the body a quarter. I am at an angle, not head-on, showing a long neck to jaw line, eyes bright, zeroed in on the camera—all that, unless your date is trying to put his arm around you, being cuddly and sweet. Then, you go for the "nice, pretty lady" look, which usually turns out boring, which everyone knows is the kiss of death—one wants to be anything and all things but boring.

Looking stylishly stunning is not for the faint of heart. Beware the Body Changer!

Food of My Life: From My Family's Table

My mother's pasta. I can see her carefully placing mounds of flour onto the large wooden cutting board. Using her hands and fingers she scoops out the center to create a round space with the flour piled high around the sides like snow-covered mountains. Next she breaks an egg and drops it on the board in the center of the circle, quickly starting the kneading process, bringing in small quantities of the flour to mix with the egg. A cup of water, brought to her by one of her children, is poured in small amounts ever so slowly as she adds more flour to the mixture. Finally, after many testings, and all the while constantly kneading the pasta dough, the ingredients are perfectly matched. With a final pat on the dough, she then begins flattening, pressing, and turning, throwing small amounts of flour on the board before each turn over. Wider and wider the circle grows under her delicate fingers; the dough becomes flatter and flatter as it spreads out, extending to the edges of the board. Then the cutting utensils, age-old cutlery passed down through the generations, are brought out from a special drawer. A small rolling wheel administered by my mother or grandmother, or by an aunt if one of them happened to knock on the kitchen door to signal a visit.

Perfect rows of noodles: raviolis cut and separated on the board for we little ones to press together around the edges with our fingers, sealing the freshly made ricotta inside.

Growing up with an awareness of the seasons—from the back porch to the garden where the cherry and peach trees filled with fruit—offered continual renewal. I remember carefully cutting the stems from the vines in the small grape arbor while holding my other hand open as the clusters of fruit dropped into it, just as my grandmother had taught me. Afterward I watched the men take the small baskets to the basement to pile the ripe fruit into the wine press. These moments were part of our lives with neighbors, family, and friends in constant flux, in and out, around and about each other's lawns and property, exchanging and passing on the abundance, so it "won't go to waste."

In many ways, our small town in Illinois was a continuation of my family's home village in Italy. A life lived by the planting, growing, and harvesting seasons. During my first visit to the old country, I accompanied my mother's stepmother (my step-grandmother) on her daily shopping trips and walkabouts. The village is in the Campania region of the peninsula, the name meaning "fertile countryside." Leaving her street, we would walk toward the park on the square where the shops were located, and as she greeted her friends, the women of the town, the inevitable conversations would center on the choices the housewives would be making to prepare and serve the midday meal. I would hear snatches of "the beef-steak for the braciola really looked good" or "not too sure about the lamb" etc., and the same sort of information about the produce at the vegetable shops was passed on. The cheese store was just as much a matter of preference as the bakery.

Both sets of my grandparents lived in the same village, several streets away from one another. Mother's family were large landowners. Father's family owned smaller pieces of property and worked the land themselves. The only way my dad would ever be able to acquire any substantial wealth— and land meant wealth to him—was to migrate. At the age of fourteen, traveling alone across the Atlantic, he joined his father in the States. America called. Factories everywhere. One dollar a day, young man. Opportunity.

And his dream came true when, in the early 40s, he purchased his farm, 326 acres of Illinois dark loam where he raised soybeans, wheat, and corn, as well as Angus beef cattle. My mother, hardly a farm girl, was happy to stay in our house on Main Street, while another family moved into the farmhouse to help dad work the farm.

For us children, the farm meant jaunts in the back of the red truck, scrambling up and grabbing onto a piece of the side rail for the ride to "the timber," the natural, wild piece of the farm, to play alongside the creek, pick blackberries for jam, and, when in season, search for the elusive morel mushrooms, which we handled ever so gently. My mother would stuff the delicate cone-shaped mushrooms and simmer them in red sauce or slice and sauté them to place alongside a T-bone. Dad would cook the T-bone on a flat, black iron skillet, turning the gas flame as high as it would go, salting the pan before placing the meat on it, and then basting the meat with dried basil and oregano stalks dipped in olive oil, quickly turning the T-bone over to baste it again.

Our lives revolve around a totally urban environment now. Two sisters and my brother live with their families spread out in cities across the country. Invariably, when we get together, our conversations turn to our growing-up days and the culture of food and style—who we were then. My younger sister, who lives not far from me and who has a community garden several blocks from her home, will invite me over for a dish of freshly prepared eggplant or sautéed rape greens in olive oil, all harvested from her tiny plot. We talk lovingly about the foods of our childhood often.

This past Thanksgiving, we decided to make ricotta from memory at my apartment. It was an amazing event. Bringing the large pot of milk to the exact boiling point, waiting for just the right amount of bubbles to appear on the surface of the milk, trying to remember exactly how many bubbles we needed before we could slowly start adding the vinegar. Watching the miracle unfold in my kitchen brought up the memories stored deep inside. I had thought a miracle was happening in my mother's kitchen as I watched her extract the creamy mounds of cheese from the milk mixture.

The food that has the deepest meaning for me was grown, prepared, and canned at our home. Tall glass jars with gold-rimmed tops, stored on shelves in the basement, held our family's tomato sauce. Those jars were special to me because I took part in the process of making the sauce.

We started with picking tomatoes from our back garden, but it had really started long before that in the early spring when I followed my grandmother up and down the freshly turned earth that my grandfather and father had prepared. My grandmother gently placed the tomato seedlings, which had been nurtured in a small hothouse at the side of the garden, in my hands, and as she drove a hole into the ground with a small wood T-shaped implement, the sharp point easily cleaving into the ground, I would drop the small stock into the hole. Then, carefully so as not to crowd the roots, my grandmother would pour water from the watering can she carried, filling the hole almost to the top. I would start packing the hole with dirt, and she would finish the process, making sure the little plant was standing straight and tall.

The entire family joined in the harvest. During picking, I habitually selected a perfectly shaped, just-the-right-size, red, plump, and warm-in-my-hands tomato. The memory of eating the fruit while standing among the rows of plants stays with me always.

Another vivid memory comes into play: sitting on low chairs or stools wrapped in grown-up aprons peeling tomatoes after they had been parboiled, with bits and pieces falling everywhere,

them off to the adults to cut and prepare them for
erent styles of sauce my mother used.

I a.. jure she knew the standard Italian names for each
style, but we children mostly learned Italian at my grandmother's knee in her native village's dialect. Years later we
would study the more formal "High Italian" that my mother
learned from the nuns at boarding school. For our benefit,
the description for sauces became "with or without seeds."
The echo of her voice floats in the air around me. "Go to the
basement," she would say, "the sauce with the seeds."

There is a disconnect, albeit a subtle one, when you distance
yourself from a life you did not fully comprehend while living
it, not thinking twice that you are leaving your tribe—and the
identity, comfort, and protection it provides—dismissing it
because one surely won't need any of that nurturing. You no
longer kneel for prayers with your sisters before bedtime, or
watch your mother finish sewing your new pinafore or sun-
dress with the matching bolero. Since you haven't considered
the strength and pull of it—how can you?—you come across it
out there, find it in your future on the way to fame and fortune.

I found myself back at my beginnings, growing up surrounded
by love, purpose, and tranquility, surrounded by extended family, a community of friends that made me what and who I am
today. To practice with absolute conviction the art of savoring
the now, acknowledging each moment before letting it pass, in
order to live with grace on this startling and brilliant earth is the
greatest gift I have taken from my family's table.

Baja and the Big Horn Desert Ram

I was staring through half-closed eyes into a swirling mass of oily liquid grit, bubbling away like molten lava erupting from a circular opening that protruded from a dry stick fire. Someone pulled the swirling mass from the glowing embers and poured the slimy black liquid into my coffee cup. Welcome to day nineteen of my desert sheep hunt.

How did it come to this? I'm bone weary, and I must look like something that comes out of a cave once every second season. I touch my cheek and grimace with pain, certain that my face is forever ruined. Jim looks over at me and says, "It'll be fine. We'll get back to Dallas and Dr. Rorwick will fix it up."

I'm wondering, is my face that bad? He's talking about a plastic surgeon friend of his. I wouldn't mind so much that the whole side of my face is black and blue if I just had my desert ram.

Lingering over my morning coffee and thinking about the fall, we get the word; it's time to move. I throw out whatever that was at the bottom of my cup, hang my canteen around my hip, and tuck my field glasses inside my shirt as Jim hands me his 7mm, trading for my .270 to take with him. "It's going to be a long shot," he said, "you'll need a heavier caliber." Always the optimist, believing that I would meet him in camp tonight with my ram, I started out on what I knew was my last hope to complete my Grand Slam.

The fall happened earlier in the three-week hunt when we made our way down a rock-strewn mountainside in Mexico's Baja Peninsula, returning to base camp after an eight-hour climb that had taken us up and over some unbelievably tough terrain, pockmarked with stiletto sharp cactus and barbed thorn trees. Hot, stumbling, crawling, and falling, we were unable to pick up any signs of sheep. One of the guides volunteered to take a walkabout, returning awhile later shaking his head as he rejoined us. We were greatly disappointed, but quickly the discussion turned to the task of getting off the mountain and onto the valley floor before dark.

One has to concentrate on every step because there are so many hidden traps, as every mountain climber knows. This country—some of the toughest in the world—demanded your total concentration. At the time of my fall, I had a nice rhythm going; there was a lovely stretch of small boulders, which enabled me to hop or step from rock to rock instead of having to crawl around them. I miscalculated a rock surface and dragged my boot, the cleat of which caught the sharp edge of a rock. I was thrown by my own weight down the side, headfirst into a boulder pile. I tried to get my hands out to break the fall, but it was too little too late. The right side of my face took the impact. I was stunned momentarily, and as Jim came to my aid, the only words I could utter were, "I broke my face, I broke my face." There was blood, and my right cheekbone was swelling like a balloon. It was the second time in one day I promised myself I would give up hunting forever.

Now, that promise unfulfilled, I am back on the mountain making a new ascent. We meet another guide and his men on our way and stop for a chat. I gather from the conversation that a borrego is somewhere down the road apiece. Great! I've been hunting these hills for eighteen days, up the mountain and down the mountain, and now I am going to take my ram off the side of the road. I think I'm going to be sick. I recognize some of the men from my former hunting party, back when life began. We talk a little back and forth; they are real sorry about my bandaged face. I personally am real sorry I ever heard of the Grand Slam for the four North American wild sheep, or of the Baja Peninsula for that matter.

I had changed guides three times. The first one was a rogue and was subsequently fired. My second guide was real good people, and now my hopes were on Ramon Aguilar, a gentleman and one of the best guides I have ever met. I could tell he was sizing me up as he approached me, and holding out his hand he greeted me with "Buenos días, Señora. So, can you shoot?"

"Yes," I replied. "I can shoot. Can you guide?" I think we both knew this day would be memorable.

Driving out past Bahía de los Ángeles into new territory, the story is relayed to me. There is indeed a ram off the side of the road, except he is straight up the side of the road about 5,000 feet. He had been spotted by the guide earlier that morning, and as it turned out, his hunter was physically unable to make the ascent. I was given the opportunity. I prayed my knees would hold out for one more climb. Mountain climbing has wrecked my knees forever; but actually, I thought, my knees can carry me: it's the rest of my body that I have slammed around for almost three weeks that might give in.

Parking our vehicle a few hundred yards down the road out of sight of the ram, we prepare for the climb. I start gathering my gear together but am told it's too soon; we are stopping for a snack. My stomach has turned to Jell-O, and they are talking about food. I nod affirmatively and am presented with a can of tuna (my 110th can of the hunt). I open it, drain the oil out onto the ground, tumble the fish onto a tortilla, roll it up and force it down. We had picked up some fresh fruit, so I have half an orange, put some beef jerky in my pocket, and I am again ready.

Ramon informs me how he would like me to take the ram. "You must take the ram with one shot, the meat is for the village, and I don't want it messed up." I told him I understand and assured him I spend hours at the shooting range, practicing, so I can do exactly that. "But," he continued, "It can be a standing shot, you may not have a rest, are you prepared?"

"Yes sir, I am prepared." Now I am worried, not of the

climb, but of messing up as he so graphically stated.

There will be four of us in the party, my new guide and two very good men. I feel more secure with the men in my troop, and lining up behind Ramon, we sally forth at 9:30 a.m. We cross a piece of flat ground and circle around some small foothills, where we are abruptly stopped by this hiss of a rattler just ahead of us and to the left. We happen to be in a narrow passage and can't see him, but we read his message loud and clear. There is no way out of this one; we have to keep going. I am already wet with perspiration as we reach the base to begin our climb up the mountain.

The pace is set for me, and we seem to stop for a rest just seconds before I have to beg a halt. The sun is directly on our backs this March day, and as we hike, there is barely scrub for shade. As I climb, my clothes and gear become unbearably heavy; the field glasses around my neck feel as though they weigh 30 pounds, and the heavy twill trousers I wear for protection feel like a suit of armor. My climbing gets slower and slower, and at every step, I have to remind myself mentally to pick up my feet. We finally stop for what I call a formal rest, which means you get to sit down if you can find a place. Ramon walks over to me, takes my rifle and shoulders it. "This rifle is for a man to carry, it is too heavy for a woman." I totally agree and will be forever grateful he toted my rifle to the top.

I still couldn't see the summit. It was straight-up noon, and the last sprint will be straight up shale rock.

I am so sick of crawling on all fours. How am I going to

get through this loose rock? I have never given up and gone back to camp, but I lift my head, stare straight at Ramon, and shake my head indicating, "No, no more." No one says a word. The men just crouch there, half-turned, looking down, and waiting for me. I can't remember ever feeling like this; I'm considering quitting, giving up and turning back. Oh, I'm not above moaning and groaning; in fact, I have spent years developing it into an art form. It's a pure craft with me.

But considering quitting is a new sensation that has to be acknowledged. I literally can't move, not down, not up. I'm scare to death of falling off this thing. I'm hot, my whole body aches, and I am bone weary. I don't know how long I stay immobile, clutching the side of that mountain, but finally, I look up. The men are still in their places, still waiting for me. I begin to move, searching for handholds, scraping and digging in footholds as I crawl up yard by yard. We inch our way to a resting place. The dreaded sensation of quitting has passed. I am relieved. I am ready.

Ramon puts his finger to his lips and gestures to shush. From now on the method of operation will be: stay low, no noise, and move fast. At this point, I am handed my rifle, one man moves out to the left, and the three of us move out to the right. We work our way around the edge of the loose shale rock while I will the soles of my boots to grip the earth, meanwhile, averting my eyes from the bottomless abyss to the right. I have no idea where the ram is or how far below us he might be; I pray that I'll have time to glass him and get a good rest. Please God, don't deal me a hand-off shot at a running sheep going away from me at 300 yards.

We sneak around safely and peer over the edge, at which time, Ramon shrugs his shoulders and my heart sinks. It's been over three hours, maybe he has left the country. Jim's 7mm is a heavier than my .270; I shift the strap to my other shoulder. There is a short conference, and we continue around, inching our way down the front face of the mountain. My body is soaked with perspiration, and the sweat is pouring down my chest and back; furthermore, perspiration is falling in my eyes, and my hands are wet on my rifle. Squatting, half-crawling, and dragging my stiff legs, my brain does a computer reboot. My mind is acutely aware, totally alert. At the same time my body is almost physically spent, my intellect has shifted up and every part of my brain is dealing only with the task at hand. The physical aspect has shifted down; the will is engaged.

I move with purpose now, hence, I have no trouble keeping up with Ramon. I'm like glue behind his huge body. My eyes are locked on to his back, watching for signals. He drops dead and drops to the ground. I do the same, and my knee rams into a needle sharp cactus spike. Nausea washes over me as I grab for my knee, tearing at my pant leg. My hand is quickly covered with blood as I try pulling out the needle, managing only to break it off. My brain has shifted again and the physical pain takes over. I want to scream. No one pays the least attention to this drama. There is nothing else to do except keep moving.

Ramon moves to the edge of an outcrop and peers over; he spots him and motions to me. There is only one place to sit, and he is in it—I shove him to the side and pull my rifle onto a rock. Looking over the edge, I scan the area; seeing only real estate, I turn to Ramon. His eyes beg me to see the ram, but the only thing he sees in mine is panic. I pull my field glasses out and scan again; I've got him. I grab my rifle and center my crosshairs on his shoulder; calculating a little over 300 yards, I pull my crosshairs up about two inches, take a breath, another one, hold it and squeeze off.

"Bueno, bueno," Ramon beams and smiles. I have completely lost the ram. I ask him, "Muerto?"

"Si, si," he answers. I try to pick him up but can't see him. Ramon and his assistants weren't moving; they just kept peering through their glasses. Then, I spot him standing. Ramon indicates I hit him in the stomach. I couldn't believe my shot had landed in his midsection. I get ready for another shot. "No, no, es muerto," he insists. My training in how one conducts themselves in the field kicks in; I prepare for the shot. At the same time, the ram turns, slowly disappearing into some shrubs. The men keep telling me, "Stay calm, just stay calm."

At that moment the realization flashes through my mind; I have to refrain myself from hitting my guide up the side of the head. It's the meat—they don't want me to mess it up. I couldn't think about that, my only concern was to dispatch a wounded animal as quickly as possible. I find my ram again, settle down, and put my crosshairs exactly where

I should have held the first time and drop him. As it turns out, he wasn't hit in the mid-section at all. My first shot was perfectly placed exactly where I had aimed, straight up his shoulder, about three inches below his back. He had been 200-225 yards away when I first saw him, and the 7mm round would not have dropped at that range.

He was a magnificent sheep; later we would measure him out at 172 points. My Grand Slam was complete, but my thoughts were only for my desert ram. I had put so much work and so much effort into this three-week odyssey, and now it was over. I was going home with my beautiful ram. Later I would dwell on the sweetness of completing my Slam—for now, the joy, exaltation, and thankfulness I feel are reserved for this animal. A completed task, what a joyous sensation. Ramon had conducted a perfect stalk that culminated in the taking of my desert ram. I knew he wasn't angry with me for taking the second shot because he took both my hands in his and then wrapped his arms around me for a beautiful hug.

When I finally got a close look at my Desert Ram, I gasped out loud; his face was scarred like mine. I slowly ran my fingers over his old battle wound. Our destiny had been determined long before this day.

Ciao, Florence

It's raining, a slow, steady, refreshing kind of rain that wakes up my sleepy self as I hurry to one of my favorite cafes in the heart of Florence.

I love the sounds of the city: the glorious church bells that ring out from dozens of church towers, reminding me to smile as I pass a gentleman playing a plaintive *'O Sole Mio* on his accordion.

The cool and sleek interior of Cavalli's coffee shop just beside the signature store became a regular hangout for my morning espresso or cappuccino, and with my morning coffee, I was treated to another unmistakable sound of the city: the clatter of cups and saucers being continually recycled as they are washed, dried and stacked. The baristas stack the smooth, white china with such flurry and style, design and balance, all the while creating symmetrical art displays.

The whole of this Etruscan city is a museum. The grand palazzos, the expansive piazzas, framed with soaring arches; public buildings designed to endure centuries, architectural elements that dazzle, fountains and sculptures abound; around every corner, another feast for the eyes as one marvels at the changing light playing on the ancient stone. Florence is alive every hour, offering Americans the perfect European street life we crave.

For years I dreamed of leasing an apartment in Florence. My beautifully furnished one bedroom was on the third floor of the Palazzo Rimbotti, each apartment lovingly decorated by the elegant Countess of the same name. I traversed Via Tornabuoni, home to Georgio Armani, Gucci, Roberto Cavalli and Hermes, which occupies the first floor of the Palazzo Rimbotti.

Leaving my street and walking toward the Ponte alle Grazie, I pass the Prada store and then Salvatore Ferragamo's headquarters, housed in a splendid, ancient, dark brownstone palazzo along the River Arno. I'm on my way to visit the Uffizi Gallery and view one more time Botticelli's *La Primavera*. I pass a performer of street art—a lone, beautiful girl encased in white—I saw her several times during my walks around the city.

On several occasions, the looming sight of Il Duomo with its huge dome provided a landmark to navigate the dozens of winding streets—the gothic, marble façade is breathtaking. Another landmark to guide me—Ponte Vecchio. The ochre tones of the shops glow. The Farmacia Santa Maria Novella, a pharmacy "antico," just off S. Maria Novella on Via della Scala enchants me. Opened in 1612, the ornate seventeenth-century building boasts a tall carved arched entryway, marble floors and fine art lining every wing, each one devoted to a single department such as perfumes, handmade soaps, and skin care. A stroll to Via de

Santo Spirito offered another memorable uniquely Florentine moment; watching the fireworks display over the Arno, in honor of Saint John, the Patron Saint of the city.

I visited jewelry designer Angela Caputi, knowing full well I probably could not afford any of her amazingly colored pieces. She was in attendance and helped me select earrings for myself as well as a bracelet for my sister, each piece between 35 and 45 Euros. Her couture collection, showcased in the Pitti Palace Costume Collection, ranges into the many thousands, but this stunning Florentine artist designs for "us" as well. I treasure the photo I had taken with her.

When one talks about Florence, for me, anyway, it comes down to the food, sensuous and sumptuous; one falls in love with its unforgettable flavors. I had a pasta dish everyday—all excellent! If I had to choose an absolute favorite, it would be from a wonderful trattoria along the river; plain large shells, made in house, with fresh, slightly cooked, pressed tomatoes, flavored with pecorino romano cheese, a drizzle of olive oil and fresh basil. I did not add grated cheese; the chef and my waiter approved. I also visited the restaurant, Buca Lapi, just around the corner from my apartment for the world famous Florentine grilled steak: a T-bone, cooked "undone."

I took a day trip north with my friend, Giuseppe, to walk along the Carrara quarries, and as I marveled at the huge marble mountains exposing their treasures, I wondered, did Michelangelo imagine David when he chose a piece of gleaming stone? Most say no. Legend has it, the master discovered his brave

David as he chipped and cut the white marble; it goes on to say the Lord himself touched his hand.

In Florence, I gazed at *David*, and when I could gaze no more, with eyes lowered, I paid homage to his maker.

Soon afterwards, I said goodbye to the stately city on the Arno.

Ciao, Firenze—

Why I Loved Stanley Marcus

Afew days after Stanley Marcus passed away at the age of 96, and while I was still getting the details and organizing myself to attend his memorial at the Dallas Symphony Hall, Kim Dawson Agency called to let me know KERA, the local public radio station, wanted me to come give a live interview on a relay with David Gardner, host of *The Motley Fool,* a radio show about CEOs and their companies. I was heartbroken about Marcus's passing but had not really had a chance to consider and dwell on what he meant to me and to so many other models that had worked for him. The interview would allow me to put into words what I had been feeling.

On the drive over to the radio station, I wept happy tears as well as sad, recalling everything relating to "Mr. Stanley." Thanks to him, I had had the opportunity to walk among the greats on the runway, some of the happiest moments of my life, but his leaving meant we were left with a huge, empty space. The world of fashion will never see his equal again. How would I describe what he meant to me, I pondered? I would start with the fact that if he had asked me to maneuver a swan dive off the roof of the store for a grand finale, it would have happened.

During the interview, I tried to convey his enormous talent, talent beyond measure. His relentless "Quest For The Best" was his guiding mission for Neiman Marcus, and when he walked through the store, everyone he passed glowed, and every display just naturally sparkled a little more. We loved him because he loved us. Mostly because he loved women! His smile as he watched us hurry to the couture floor for a designer show was all we needed to spur us to do our best. He transformed Dallas into a cosmopolitan city by bringing the world to Neiman Marcus.

He was, above all, a gentleman, a term, as the radio host pointed out, that is "infrequently used" today. Mr. Stanley carried himself with grace, entering a room with a twinkle in his eye, displaying intelligence and humor; he didn't attempt to bombard everyone with his presence. He insisted on the best service whether the customer was buying a $10 item or spending thousands.

During a book tour for his 1979 book, *Quest for the Best*, *People* magazine did a story on Mr. Stanley. He named the best bottled water (Evian), the best taxi (the black elegant cabbies that ply the streets of London), and the best American designer (James Galanos). The two-page, centerfold photo for the article highlights the elegant Stanley Marcus standing in front of one of the famous cabs and me, seated, posing on the hood in a magnificent red Galanos gown.

All the while the photographer was clicking away I was praying: please keep this $8,000 gown from harm's way. Model's worst nightmare: damaged merchandise. Accidents happen of course, and you are forgiven, but any careless handling, resulting in a possible streak across my backside as I slid off the cabbie, would not be deemed an accident, but a gross disregard for the garment. So, I did the only thing I could do, steadied myself on the bumper and took a flying leap off the thing.

Thanks to Mr. Stanley, I have been backstage with many of the top designers of our time. Karl Lagerfeld once accessorized me backstage at the Majestic Theatre in Dallas, prior to presenting his collection for Neiman Marcus. There was Karl, assuring each of us how beautiful we were while completing the finishing touches before our calls. When asked about Marcus's legacy, I said he made shopping like theater! He made it glamorous, a wonderful event.

His lofty position is secure in the international select club of men and women listed as "Arbiters of Taste."

In the *People* interview, for his *Quest For The Best* tour, Marcus responded to the question, "What is the goal for any retailer?" His answer, one word: "Mystique." He went on to say, "You can't buy it at any price, and the best publicist can't build it. It must be based on truth. Bendel's has it, Bonwit's didn't. Judy Garland had one, Barbara Streisand doesn't. St. Laurent had it, Cardin doesn't. Abercrombie & Fitch had, but lost, it. Gloria Vanderbilt has always had it, Charlotte Ford never had it. Sophia Loren has held on to it, Gina Lollabrigida never attained one. Jackie O had one, but blew it. The Yankees have had one and kept it."

So to you, Mr. Stanley, a gentleman in every way, thank you for letting me orbit around in your incomparable sphere of style.

Helen Martin's Style Philosophy

Women + Glamour. The two things that should never be considered apart. Together, they are the pillars of my style philosophy. All women are equal before the law of glamour. So be bold, be brave, be uniquely you.

It's about having fun while creating your own personal style. Start with the shades and tones and colors of our universe.

Bill Blass, one of the great American couture designers, whom I modeled for in the 70s and 80s, famously said, "When in doubt, wear red."

Color and more color—all the Brights you have ever loved—gather them up and include them in your life.

And while we're at it, have fun!

At a certain age some women begin to feel the glamorous part of their life is over—Nonsense! I reject the following notions that women tend to embrace as they grow older. As in:

- Must appear sensible and responsible at all times, dress conservatively, don't be daring, alluring, sensual, etc. etc.

- You can't wear that, you're too tall.

- I'm too old to wear my hair long. Find a hair stylist who will help you maintain it. Hair does not have to be a burden.

- Skinny jeans? Oh, I couldn't do that.

- I can't wear hats.

- False eyelashes? Come on!

- Dresses that actually fit the curves of my body—too scary.

My make-up essentials: Lightly bronze your face, add glow just above your cheekbones, and don't forget to add a touch of white eye shadow at the spot just between your nose and your eyelid. Great in evening light, and a must if the paparazzi are aiming a camera your way. It happens; be ready, please. I can hear you lamenting, "But I never go out!" Stop it. What about attending a charity benefit or fundraising dinner for your favorite nonprofit? That outfit you have been saving, the one that is too dressy for upscale casual, pull it out of the back of the closet, mix yourself a "dressing drink" and start finding your glamour. Movie theaters, even in small cities, have movie premiers; many times all you need is a ticket to walk the red carpet. What about openings for new shopping venues? The local press will cover these ventures, and often retail companies hire professional photographers. Ditto for charity events. My point is: go out! Speaking of photographs—what about those selfies you and your girlfriends took at your birthday party? That moment will never come back; none of those moments will.

Of course, mascara is a must, and if you like, apply a light layer of false eyelashes and play around with some smoky charcoal eyeshadow. Alluring, mysterious, glamorous. Top off that glorious face with your coral/pink or true red lip colors. Do it now!

Whatever dress size we wear, it doesn't matter. Most of us need some kind of alteration because *in dressing, it's all about the fit!* If it's a pencil skirt, make sure it fits snugly (not tight) and tapers to below the knee. Google: Marilyn Monroe pencil skirt. Fits snugly, not too tight. It's called sensual glamour. Trying to look "sexy" in a too-tight anything is not authentic.

And do stop with those tiny, cut-off raggedy shorts that fit like underpants on your bottom. Choose tailored shorts that fit well and look sporty, smart, and sleek. Wear them with a great bold tee, blouse, or shirt. Wear a pair of sporty shorts with a bomber jacket, a blazer; add a smart shoe boot or short bootie.

Sundresses are wonderful, but, sorry, we don't like to see those long things, generally in cheap fabrics that drag the floor, while walking the mall in stupid flip flops at 10:00 a.m. in the morning. Did you sleep in that?

Speaking of inappropriate apparel, Karl Lagerfeld said it best: "Sweatpants are a sign of defeat. You lost control of your life so you bought some sweatpants."

Jeans and swimsuits—toughest fits, depressing try-ons, and still can't find what you want. I wrote an article for

Today's Dallas Women magazine on the subject; allow me to quote the opening paragraph:

> For we women of a certain age, those two words conjure up horrible images of fitting-room battles; pulling on; taking off, trying to put on; calling for help to get it off. Finally after we have tried on every suit or pair of jeans in the store, spent a couple of hours wrestling with clothes that SHOULD fit, we call a truce, back away from the three-way-mirror, change into our street clothes and wave good-bye to the size 4, 5'10" sales associate, with whatever is left of our dignity and wait to fight another day.

That scenario does not ever have to happen again because you are not going to try on a dozen different swimsuits, only certain styles. Depending on your age and body type, there are some one-piece suits out there that may work for you. I prefer the ones that have a built-in thingy that cinches the waist. I have given up on the one-piece since I discovered the "Tankini." The fitted bra, tank top style falls over your tummy and covers the small of your back, but leaves a little skin showing above the bikini bottom. Perfect!

Jeans, JEANS, Jeans! Where does one start? What and how you wear your jeans has nothing to do with your age. I don't think about age when dressing because if I did think about dressing *for my age*, that process would become a big bore; let's see, I'm fifty now, so I can't wear that now. Oh, wait, I'm sixty, so I can't wear that. You see where that goes—nowhere.

I have seen seventy and eighty year old women looking fabulous in jeans. Why? Because they fit well. Jeans are the greatest invention ever! We love the look of a great pair of jeans.

Go for the low-riders ONLY if you cannot see bulges scrunched up over the beltline. I am trying to be gentle here. If that happens when you try on those very low-waist styles, then simply try on jeans that have a natural waistline. Personally, I have slim hips, but my waistline is trying to match them, so my brilliant alteration woman removes the waist band, cuts it in the back, adds a 1-2 inch piece of fabric, and puts the whole thing back together. Presto—no bulges! If you tend to be hippy or curvy, do not wear jeans that taper to hug your leg around the ankle. The balance is thrown out of proportion, and your hips will become the focal point, appearing larger than they really are.

I will only say this word once: 'leggings,' the new curse of inappropriate dressing. Do not listen to the sales associate telling you "you can wear them with so many different tops." THEY ARE TIGHTS. If they look like tights, feel like tights, if they hug every inch of your hips, tummy, bottom and legs, then THEY ARE TIGHTS.

"Fashions fade, style is eternal."
—Yves Saint Laurent

What about seasonal dressing? Is it still alive and well? Not really. It is almost a thing of the past. Gabardine and wools are worn all year round, and leather has become a non-seasonal staple. Short leather skirts look great with tights and a fitted sweater. When spring comes around, wear with bare legs and a great tee.

One of the most interesting ways to make a personal statement is in your use of accessories. Do not underestimate the important "look" of a great scarf, strategically placed and styled, or a stole, a long fringed shawl, a bold gold cuff on the wrist. Or, finesse your outfit with a fantastic belt. Years ago I bought a Michael Kors leather belt in taupe. Extraordinary designer—I modeled in one of his shows in the 80s. I still wear that belt, soft wide supple leather that fits around the hips like a peplum. Style is eternal.

I am frequently asked if I had only one piece of advice to give that would help women achieve a strong image and their own sense of style. The answer would be . . . Posture.

All those reminders our mothers used to say over and over: Sit up straight, don't slouch, stand up straight, hold your head up. She was right, so let's try it—

Standing straight, knees slightly bent, tummy pulled in as you lift your ribcage out of your waist. While your arms and hands fall naturally along your sides, think long neck, with chin parallel to the floor. Good work!

Using your thigh muscles and core muscles (remember yoga classes), move with purpose as you glide across the floor. Beautiful!

Proper posture helps you feel confident and gives you the

assurance to walk into a room and claim your space. The confidence to hesitate, just a moment; let your eyes take in the room and faces, and then move wherever you choose, only after your presence has been appreciated.

"Attitude is everything."
—Diane Von Furstenberg

Naturally, you are skilled in verbal communication, taking what you need from an encounter, not wasting their time or yours, giving an assuring smile to a friend or a stranger, dispensing a friendly touch, a look to let everyone you encounter realize they are special, because you know, *we are all special.*

While we always should express and practice intellectual curiosity, when the hammer meets the nail, the most important trait we humans can offer one another is the gift of impeccable manners.

You are goodness and light every minute of every day. No one has your essence, your spirit, and your beautiful self. Celebrate yourself!

"You can have anything you want in life if you dress for it."
—Edith Head

Advertisement for Titches' Holiday Jewelry, Dallas, Texas

Photograph by Constance Ashley

Photograph by Jeannette Korab

Photograph by Constance Ashley, Dallas, Texas

Retrospective Fashion Show for Hollywood designer, Edith Head

Acknowledgments

Thank you to the following publications for printing the original versions of: "Africa Lost" (*Sports Afield*, Special Classic Issue, October 2016); "Hunting by Moonlight" and "¡Viva Hispania!" (*KYH Magazine*, Shikar Safari Club, 1989); "My Baja Ram" (*Petersen's Hunting*, September 1987); and "*Ciao*, Florence" (*FD Magazine*, November 2014).

I want to thank: my brilliant editor Sarah Theobald-Hall who kept me on the right track with suggestions to go further, dig deeper, furnishing me with expert advice, clarity of purpose and insightful comments. My sister Lou Michaels whose suggestions on theme and placement helped define the character of the book. My dear friend, author, editor, and writing instructor, Jill Sayre who edited early versions of two essays in the book. Her critiques of all the pieces of my work that she reviews, while in various writing groups, always prove invaluable.

My thanks to all my family and friends, especially my sister Angela Cross and brother Andrew Ippolito for their steadfast support.

And many heartfelt thanks to my publisher Ted Ruybal and all the staff at Wisdom Books for their patience, advice, and wisdom. I especially I want to acknowledge Ted's brilliant expertise in guiding the book through to completion.

My grateful acknowledgment to the wonderful world that is KD Conservatory, College of Film and Dramatic Arts, my second home for many years. A thousand thanks to President Kathy Tyner for her encouragement and support.

About the Author

Photograph by Constance Ashley,
makeup Gi Gi Coker

Helen Martin rose to prominence as a high fashion runway model in the rarefied world of couture while becoming equally successful as a commercial and fashion photographer's model. During the mid 1990s, she was the inexhaustible Style Editor for *Today's Dallas Woman*, authoring lifestyle articles as well as producing monthly fashion features. Her essays more recently have appeared in national publications such as *FD Magazine* and *Sports Afield*. Currently, her professional home is KD Conservatory, College of Film and Dramatic Arts, where she helps young people in the entertainment industry achieve their dreams. Ms. Martin is busy working on her second book; a memoir devoted to her grandmother Caterina and her mother Maria. Their story begins in a provincial town in Italy at the end of the nineteenth century. And, she is always looking for the next Red Carpet to walk.

CPSIA information can be obtained
at www.ICGtesting.com
Printed in the USA
LVHW041108090520
654944LV00006B/686